WHAT'S BECOME OF CULTURAL STUDIES?

GRAEME TURNER

SAGE

Los Angeles | London | New Delhi
Singapore | Washington DC

SAGE Publications Ltd
1 Oliver's Yard
55 City Road
London EC1Y 1SP

SAGE Publications Inc.
2455 Teller Road
Thousand Oaks, California 91320

SAGE Publications India Pvt Ltd
B 1/I 1 Mohan Cooperative Industrial Area
Mathura Road, Post Bag 7
New Delhi 110 044

SAGE Publications Asia–Pacific Pte Ltd
33 Pekin Street #02–01Far East Square
Singapore 048763

Library of Congress Control Number: 2011923545

British Library Cataloguing in Publication data

A catalogue record for this book is available from the British Library

ISBN 978–1–84920–583–2
ISBN 978–1–84920–584–9 (pbk)

Typeset by C&M Digitals (P) Ltd, Chennai, India
Printed in India by Replika Press Pvt. Ltd
Printed on paper from sustainable resources

CONTENTS

ABOUT THE AUTHOR

Graeme Turner is Australian Research Council Federation Fellow and Director of the Centre for Critical and Cultural Studies at the University of Queensland in Brisbane, Australia. He is one of the founding figures of cultural studies in Australia, and a major contributor to the field internationally; his *British Cultural Studies: An Introduction* (1990, 1996a, 2003) was the first book to provide an overview of cultural studies for an international readership. In addition to his involvement in debates around the theory and practice of cultural studies, he has published on a wide range of topics within cultural and media studies, and on a variety of media – film, television, radio and the press. His work on celebrity (*Fame Games: The Production of Celebrity in Australia* [2000]), co-authored with Frances Bonner and P. David Marshall, and *Understanding Celebrity* [2004]) is widely cited as among the foundational contributions to this emerging field. His most recent book, *Ordinary People and the Media: The Demotic Turn* (2010), focused on the increasing prominence of 'ordinary people' in the media, and examines the politics that might be seen to generate that prominence. Graeme Turner's current research project is a large transnational study of television in the post-broadcast era, which has involved comparative work in Asia and Latin America; publications so far include (co-edited with Jinna Tay) *Television Studies after TV: Understanding Television in the Post-Broadcast Era* (2009).

ACKNOWLEDGEMENTS

This book has a list of acknowledgements which is a little more extensive than customary for me because, more directly than any of my previous publications, it has developed out of numerous exchanges and debates with my cultural studies colleagues. Indeed, the idea for this book originally came out of a series of conversations with my friend and publisher, Chris Rojek, who raised the initial proposition and has been an enthusiastic supporter of the project as it has developed and mutated into its current form.

I wrote the first half of the book while I was a guest of the Scholars' Program in Communication and Culture at the Annenberg School for Communication at the University of Pennsylvania in Philadelphia in 2010. My stay there was one of the most pleasurable and stimulating experiences I have had and I am extremely grateful to the wonderful Barbie Zelizer for the invitation and for her generosity and friendship while I was there. A number of the Annenberg community assisted me with thinking about the book through colloquia presentations and private conversations; among those with whom I most enjoyed talking over the four months there are Marwan Kraidy, Katherine Sender, Joe Turow, Michael X. Delli Carpini, Elihu Katz, Monroe Price, and my Scholar's Program colleague, Melani McAlister. Emily Plowman was a tireless and engaging support system for the programme and for Melani and myself.

Several friends and colleagues have read sections of the draft, but the ones who read the most, and who were therefore most generous with their time and in their comments and suggestions, are Meaghan Morris and Michael Delli Carpini, and I want to thank them for their contribution to the final product. My colleague and research collaborator at the Centre for Critical and Cultural Studies, Anna Pertierra, has generously read drafts of several chapters for me while being, as always, an astute and insightful sounding board for ideas as they have developed.

This book has been the focus of many conversations which may not have been particularly notable to those concerned but were nonetheless extremely valuable to me as I tested ideas and sought more information. Among those who I would like to acknowledge for their help in this way are Mark Andrejevic, Anne Balsamo, Michael Bérubé, Charlotte Brunsdon, Nick Couldry, Melissa Gregg, Larry Grossberg, Gay Hawkins, James Hay, Chris Healy, Toby Miller, Elspeth Probyn, David Shumway, and Sue Turnbull.

Some parts of some chapters have been published in earlier versions and so I thank the editors of *Cultural Studies Review* and of *Cultural Studies* for their permission to make use of that material. I also wish to thank Duke University Press and Larry Grossberg for permission to reproduce the quotation used as the epigraph for Chapter 6. The team at SAGE, particularly Jai Seaman, has been excellent to deal with over the course of the writing and its production.

My wife, Chris, who has lived with the everyday presence of the project of cultural studies longer than most of those who get paid to do so, has as always been a sustaining force and a necessary antidote to the more testing aspects of academic work.

Finally, the regular work in progress sessions in my own workplace, the Centre for Critical and Cultural Studies at the University of Queensland, and the astute, intelligent and generous input from what is absolutely the most wonderful group of academic colleagues one could wish for, have played a significant part in shaping the approach and the arguments made. Of course, none of those named are to blame for any of what follows; these are my views but I am grateful for the help I have had in forming them.

Graeme Turner
Brisbane, February, 2011

INTRODUCTION: PRACTISING CULTURAL STUDIES TODAY

I

At the third international Crossroads of Cultural Studies conference, hosted at the legendary point of origin, Birmingham's Centre for Contemporary Cultural Studies, in 2000, the Anglo-American expansion of cultural studies was probably at its peak. There were 800 papers organized in 11 parallel sessions across three days. Many of these papers revealed the influence of the key fashion of the day – largely, sophisticated textual analyses in the service of identity politics. An often repeated story, perhaps apocryphal but nonetheless still resonant, has it that one of the founding fathers of cultural studies, when leafing through his copy of the book of abstracts (a sizable object) after he arrived at the conference, was heard to ask, sadly: 'Is this what we have become?'

This anecdote circulated at the time, mostly, but possibly not solely, as a provocation for private discussions of just what it was that people thought cultural studies *had* become. More than a decade on, this book argues, the consideration of what has become of cultural studies is now of some urgency. What this book sets out to do, however, is not to continue the work of theoretical clarification that was so fundamental to cultural studies in its early years; nor will it attempt to resolve those disciplinary debates that have continued to mark its histories – the role of political economy, say, or the rolling definition of what counts as cultural studies and what does not. Rather, its task is the slightly more pragmatic one of examining certain aspects of the practice of cultural studies as it has become more institutionally established: its behaviours now more like those of the disciplines it was set up to trouble, many of its current practitioners (for one reason or another) seemingly more invested in their professional careers, and much of both its teaching and research revealing what this book will describe as an increasing complacency about cultural studies' usefulness, applications and effects.

This is a field about which its most respected theorist is quoted as having said recently, 'I think it contains a lot of rubbish' (this was Stuart Hall in his *New Humanist* interview with Laurie Taylor in 2006). There was no roar of protest at such a comment. This might raise the suspicion that it is generally, if perhaps only tacitly, acknowledged by many of those in the field that cultural studies actually *does* contain 'a lot of rubbish'. If this is so, then perhaps those of us who identify with cultural studies need to talk about this as a problem to be considered, understood and dealt with.

This book offers a personal accounting of what, in my view, cultural studies has become in order to provoke debate within the field: it asks if cultural studies has really managed to maintain a connection with its original political, ethical and pedagogical mission at the same time as it has contributed to the recent expansion of the fields of research, theory and debate within the humanities and social sciences usually collected under titles such as 'the new humanities' or, sometimes, 'theory'. My account highlights what the achievement of cultural studies has been, before pointing to things that seem to have gone, or perhaps are in the process of going, wrong. The ambition of the book is to redirect debate in cultural studies by presenting some honest home truths about where we are and what we should do about it.

Given the territory I am entering here, and given that I have no illusions about how contentious this territory is, I should make very clear what I think this book is *not*. This book is *not* an attack on the idea of cultural studies, a nostalgic call for a return to some golden age of cultural studies, or a veiled critique of the influence of particular individuals or schools of thought on cultural studies theory. Rather, it is an attempt to take an honestly critical look at what the practice of cultural studies has become, for many of us, in many places, for much of the time, and to ask – is this, really, what we had in mind?

II

Let me start with a series of rhetorical questions for the reader to consider. What is it like to work in cultural studies today? When we go to a cultural studies conference, is it packed with interesting papers doing challenging things in the service of a common intellectual project? Or are they more likely to be wearyingly predictable, with many of the same old theoretical vehicles, albeit fashionably customized to their owners' personal tastes, being driven around small sectors of familiar terrain. Perhaps they will be clever readings of the latest 'quality' offering from HBO, or user-generated video on YouTube; or they may be audience studies or 'ethnographies' examining a tiny sample's response to the latest reality television format; or, increasingly likely today, they could be free-associating predictions of the impact of the latest new technology on old (or 'legacy') media and the public sphere; or, and finally, maybe they will present accounts of changes within the cultural industries or the media policy environment that are apparently disinterested in any historical information that precedes the mid-1990s. A little harsh, you think, this list of possibilities? Or, are they depressingly familiar?

Let's consider another context for the practice of cultural studies. How about those of us who have to assess competitive research applications: how many of these are exciting for their ambition and their likely impact, and how many are merely offering the state (or sometimes the private fund) the opportunity to invest in the performative application of a currently fashionable theorist's approach to a new, 'surprisingly neglected', body of texts or practices?

Or, more worryingly, how do we feel when we witness younger scholars, with their freshly minted PhDs and ambitions of making a difference, being encouraged through the blogo-sphere and elsewhere to seize their opportunities to become 'public intellectuals' straight away – on the back of one com-pleted research project, a sincere commitment to cultural stud-ies, an incipient sense of history, a continuing institutional position, and access to a computer?

Of course, I know that such talk mimics, disturbingly, the kinds of things that are said about cultural studies by its ene-mies: by the pundits and politicians and academics from other disciplines who like to describe cultural and media studies as the trendy and superficial nadir of academic endeavour. But what if there is a kernel of truth even in some of this – not in terms of the scepticism about the project of cultural studies, but in terms of what it has (unwittingly, or carelessly or compla-cently) enabled to happen in its name? We couldn't easily admit such a thing publicly without providing ammunition to those who would happily shoot the whole field down, and for whom fine distinctions between the value of individual projects within the field would be irrelevant. However, perhaps that has come to mean that we are reluctant to admit such misgivings pri-vately, even among ourselves, despite the fact that it is simply routine for many of us (most of us?) to leave a conference feel-ing that it has been on balance a waste of time, that the whole field is clearly going to the dogs, and lamenting the frustration of listening to people innocently reinvent a wheel, the prior existence of which might have been revealed by a little more thorough, disciplined and patient research. Admitting such pos-sibilities as the subject for close enquiry is the provocation I want to lay out in this introduction as a means of setting up the chapters that follow.

III

I work in Australia, but over my career I have studied, taught or occupied visiting positions in the UK, the USA, Canada, Hong Kong, Taiwan and Austria. Much of what I have to say I hold to be true of cultural studies as a field, and not just of the Australian (or British or American) iteration of it. There are important specificities, however, in how cultural studies has played out around the world and I can't pretend to be well informed about all of them. Where I am aware of significant exceptions to my arguments I will note these; however, I am not going to pepper the sentences that follow with lists of inclusions and exceptions on every point. In general, what I am going to describe is what I judge to be tendencies that are sufficiently widespread to justify talking about them as representative. I am comfortable with the fact that the reader is going to make their own judgements about how representative these tendencies are in relation to their own specific location and conditions. The purpose of the book is to generate debate about the state of cultural studies today, and it is entirely appropriate that the reader should be in an active engagement with its arguments, assessing just how valid they are as accounts of their particular circumstances. That said, I think what I have to say in what follows does speak to those working in cultural studies in most places where it happens, about practices that are important in most places where it happens, and addresses concerns that have been expressed by many of those practising cultural studies, again, in most places where it happens.

There is a danger, of course, in this kind of project, particularly when one is a card-carrying member of the first generation of cultural studies scholars. Speaking honestly is no guarantee that you won't be misunderstood, and I recognize that at least some of what follows might be read as a nostalgic lament. For what it's worth, that is not how I think of it. Rather, my concern is for the future, for the long-term survival of what I think of, on balance, as the discipline of cultural studies. At the centre of that concern is the situation of younger researchers entering the field. From what I see around me, there is much greater professional pressure on these young people than I faced at the beginning of my career: there are high expectations for their professional performance, more intrusive and bureaucratized scrutiny in the workplace, a shrinking division between their work and their private lives, and more just plain angst about their careers. It is largely through witnessing their difficulties at close quarters over the past five years, as I have led a national research network that has prioritized the needs of early career researchers, that I have become aware of how poorly we have prepared many of these people for the roles they have to play. It seems that this is particularly the case for cultural studies and my view, influencing much of what is said in what follows, is that there are identifiable causes that can be addressed. After all, this is a problem which is to do with the cultural practices that shape everyday working lives, precisely the domain to which cultural studies is most sensitive.

The other prefatory comment I should make is that while I don't want to get ensnared within any of the familiar debates about 'what is cultural studies', I am aware that underpinning what I say in these chapters will be an implicit model of what cultural studies is for me. I don't want to spend any part of this book defending that model – that is not my purpose here. However, neither do I want to exnominate it. So, let me admit that the model of cultural studies I have in play here has the following features. It sees cultural studies as a conjunctural practice that is intrinsically interdisciplinary; while it is grounded in the body of theory that has developed as a result of the project of cultural studies and in particular the early work from Birmingham and the traditions flowing from it, it is also genuinely engaged in working across disciplinary and transnational territories which were not necessarily part of that history. This is a version of cultural studies which, notwithstanding its early investment in textual analysis and questions of representation, has no qualms about making use of empirical research methods, or the approaches of political economy that informed so much early work in media and communications studies, cultural policy studies and media history. It is not, though, interested in mere description; it is critical and concerned with its contribution to the public good. There is obviously much more that could be said here, but this at least takes the covers off so that what 'my cultural studies' looks like can be seen.

Let me now summarize the focus of each of the following chapters. Chapter 1, 'The Achievements of Cultural Studies', commences by engaging in a selective stock-take of what we might claim so far as the achievements of cultural studies. No surprises here, perhaps, but it does seem important that a book like this makes clear claims for the value of what cultural studies has been able to do. Not only would I argue that it has exercised an influence within the university, but I would also argue it has had an impact on the character of public discourse: it is notable how many concepts that originated in cultural studies have become part of the way culture is now talked about in the media, in politics and in policy frameworks. More centrally, the institutional success of cultural studies – where this has occurred – demands attention, despite (or, maybe, because of) the long-running debates about this kind of achievement within cultural studies itself. I will also argue that cultural studies rescued everyday life and popular culture from the neglect of the traditional disciplines and placed them at the centre of contemporary academic enquiry and research. Along the way, it opened up a number of disciplines (such as film studies, for one) to new approaches and perspectives that have proved dramatic in their impact.

Any moves towards constructing a triumphalist narrative about the establishment of cultural studies as a discipline must, however, be constrained by the cold fact that cultural studies is, in principle and in practice, actively ambivalent about disciplinarity. On the one hand, cultural studies is responsible for a major assault on disciplinarity as part of its original project, but, on the other hand, now that it has matured as a field and in its institutional habitus, cultural studies does tend to behave very much like a discipline itself – albeit without some of the more rigorous protocols an explicit acknowledgement of this would entail. Nonetheless, it is not unusual for those working in cultural studies to continue to reject the idea of disciplinarity for their field in order to highlight instead the political and critical benefits that come from their 'un-disciplined' stance.

In reality, it seems to me now (notwithstanding the fact that I have been as eager as anyone else to take this position myself in the past), such a position is not much more than an affectation, its flimsiness revealed when we look at the content of undergraduate courses where there is usually plenty of evidence of a discipline being taught. The affectation is not without significant, and I would argue deleterious, consequences. Curriculum design at undergraduate level as well as the disciplinary preparation received by graduate students – especially those working within the British model (the UK, Australia, New Zealand, for instance) where there is no substantial programme of coursework – is certainly disciplinary in its thematic orientation and frame of reference, but less so in the inculcation of standards of research, argument and criticism. What this means is that it has the negative aspects of a discipline – its sense of boundaries – without enough of the positives, that is, a fully developed epistemology that can be taught as method. Chapter 2, 'The Undiscipline: Cultural Studies and Interdisciplinarity'. argues that among the problems in contemporary cultural studies is the lack of precisely the disciplinary training the first generation of cultural studies scholars benefited from because they came from the traditional disciplines – before then rejecting disciplinarity. The current generation must be content with the consequences of that rejection rather than themselves experiencing the grounds for it. Finally, it is also the case that the claims for 'un-disciplinarity' may just simply end up as a complacent fiction that does not any longer accurately describe what has become of cultural studies. To think more about that, we need to turn to the subject of the next chapter, teaching cultural studies.

Teaching has not been at the forefront of discussions in the Western formations of cultural studies over the past decade, even though, certainly in the case of the UK and Australia, it was through teaching programmes at graduate and undergraduate level that cultural studies demonstrated its value to the universities concerned. As research has become a more significant driver of university investment, and as cultural studies in the USA has become institutionally consolidated around research interests rather than teaching programmes, it would be fair to say that in general the focus has shifted to cultural studies research, with teaching receding into the background.

Chapter 3, 'Teaching Cultural Studies', argues that the teaching of cultural studies has changed in ways that render it vulnerable to the accusation that it has become as elitist, as canonical, and as mystificatory as those disciplines it was set up to displace – such as literary studies. Beginning with a discussion of cultural studies teaching in Australia that will resonate with those teaching it elsewhere, this chapter examines the extent to which we need to remind ourselves of the original attributes of cultural studies teaching – such as its respect for and interest in the cultural knowledges and experiences of its students.

One of the key cultural studies debates in the early 1990s was provoked by the surge in optimistic readings of all kinds of media texts, aimed at demonstrating how audiences might resist dominant readings, and even generate their own, oppositional, readings of mainstream popular texts. These approaches developed in response to what, in the 1980s, had become something of an Althusserian orthodoxy that encouraged overly deterministic analyses of the processes of culture. While welcomed as a necessary corrective in many circles at the time, this form of interpretation was also criticized for being too complacent about the power of the audience to resist that of the media and, ultimately, of capital. It was accused of cultural populism – of pandering to already established cultural preferences among cultural studies academics by examining only those popular texts and practices that were open to such optimistic interpretations: transgressive television, spectacular subcultures and so on (see McGuigan, 1992).

In my book *Ordinary People and the Media: The Demotic Turn* (2010), I suggested that there was a new version of this cultural populism, and it has arisen in relation to the analysis of developments in new media. While there is certainly much of importance to deal with in the explosion of digital media, I have argued that the dominant accounts have exaggerated its likely political effects (as well as the likely industrial effects). Not only that, I also argued that this has been influenced by the writers' own investment in, and their naïve acceptance of the media industries' own spin on, these new developments. Much of this work has its roots in cultural studies, even those accounts which remain explicitly aligned with the efforts of capital to turn those new technologies into profitable businesses. It is claimed that the roots of the creative industries brand – now a key location for the discussion of new media – lie in cultural studies even though in many ways its interests and objectives run in opposite directions. The principles of privatization, entrepreneurialism and individualism are anathema, I would have thought, to cultural studies thinking; but they are fundamental to the creative industries paradigm. The buzz words of innovation and creativity have linked research and teaching in the creative industries with what has become a surprisingly unproblematic alignment with the developmental needs of business through a spurious invocation of the promise of community or 'democratic' empowerment.

Chapter 4, 'Unintended Consequences: Convergence Culture, New Media Studies and Creative Industries' examines what cultural studies has become from the perspectives offered by these new fields because in some locations now they occupy the space once occupied by cultural studies. Much of that is teaching space, inhabited by the very same kind of student who would once have turned to cultural studies for excitement – or else would have been attracted by their interest in the professional outcomes linked with these programmes, such as careers in journalism or media production (this, of course, is what helped cultural studies in the beginning as well). In these, largely institutional, terms, we may be approaching something of a crisis for cultural studies as in some locations it is struggling to retain the territory established in the 1990s against competition from these more contemporary initiatives. The worrying question this chapter investigates, however, is whether they have sufficient theoretical and disciplinary substance, whether they are simply the product of an academic rebranding exercise, and whether they have much to do with cultural studies traditions at all.

Chapter 5, 'Internationalizing Cultural Studies: From Diaspora to Indigeneity' turns its attention to the internationalization of cultural studies. The spread of cultural studies, largely but not solely, emanates from the UK, of course, initially as a diasporic formation when many British cultural studies academics fled Thatcher's Britain in search of greener pastures. Their influence in Australia, Canada, New Zealand and the USA has been profound, although in different ways and for different reasons in each instance. In all the Anglophone contexts, however, much of the early local work reflects a significant input from British expatriates, and in many cases referred back to the equivalent of a theoretical homeland. While the British influence was substantially enabling, it didn't necessarily assist in the production of an indigenized or locally inflected version of cultural studies in the various locations. Whereas Australia was quick to develop such a version, for a variety of reasons, Canada, for one, took much longer. New Zealand is arguably still to do this. In all cases, these developments incorporated some myths of origins that inevitably privileged the British tradition. For many years, it has to be said also, cultural studies was very much an Anglo-American project, with minimal penetration into the European university system or into Asia.

Increasingly since the early 1990s, however, we have seen cultural studies migrate into non-Anglo locations where the Britishness of cultural studies is not taken for granted, nor necessarily embraced or accepted. The work of new formations such as Inter-Asia Cultural Studies, for instance, explicitly sets itself against such a history in an attempt to remake cultural studies for the contexts in which it is to be used. What this has done is to reaffirm the conjunctural nature of the best cultural studies can do. While much of the discussion about the internationalization of cultural studies has so far concentrated on its adoption within the USA, this chapter attempts to widen the frame to focus on new uses for cultural studies that are emerging as it is taken up outside the Anglophone West.

My concluding chapter asks, 'Does Cultural Studies have a Future?'. The institutional context in the various locations will ultimately determine this, of course, but if cultural studies is to survive and continue to contribute in a valuable and critical way, at least three key developments are required: (i) reviving a core attribute I argue has fallen away, (ii) a broadening of its interdisciplinary purchase; and (iii) a commitment to its disciplinary future. In the case of the first development, the critical mission and everyday relevance of cultural studies has been submerged in much cultural studies teaching, as well as by some of the newer expressions of the field, such as creative industries and new media studies. It is important that what matters about cultural studies is brought back to the fore: that is, a critical mission that has a political and moral purpose, which is about the public good before economic development, and which addresses the issues of the cultural distribution of power as a core concern. The global financial crisis has shown us once again the necessity for such perspectives to regain an influence over the public sphere.

The second development reinforces what is already under way in some locations; that is, to exploit further the developmental capacities of cultural studies as a genuinely interdisciplinary research field within the humanities and social sciences. Drawing on the experience of the Australian-based Cultural Research Network (CRN), which I convened, this chapter argues that cultural studies can serve as a kind of academic *lingua franca* for the new humanities, a common theoretical and methodological language which may enable those disciplines engaged in cultural research to work with each other. That is an appropriate objective for an 'undiscipline' interested in continuing the project of reshaping the disciplinary terrain of the humanities and social sciences. It is not, however, sufficient on its own because the survival of cultural studies, I argue – and this is the third development – fundamentally depends on a serious institutional commitment to maintaining it as an identifiable disciplinary field. Finally, in this chapter, a concluding section reviews the arguments made throughout the book, which point to the renovations necessary to 'what's become of cultural studies' so that it has a future which responds to the promise of its pasts.

THE ACHIEVEMENTS OF CULTURAL STUDIES

I was among the first (admittedly, of many) to write a book length account of the development of cultural studies (Turner, 1990, 1996a, 2003); the point of my doing this at that time was to try to make cultural studies approaches accessible to a broader readership than those who were going to be reading *Working Papers in Cultural Studies* or the various readers being published through Hutchison, the Open University and so on. Today, the idea of cultural studies still seems to me as important and as relevant as it ever has been. However, what has *happened* to this idea in practice – how it has been implemented in various contexts, what kinds of influence it has had, and ultimately where I worry that it may have lost some of its power – is the topic of this book.

Obviously, there could be quite a bit of debate about what follows – both from inside and outside the cultural studies tent. Indeed, generating debate is one of the objectives of this book. What I would like to do first, however, before properly commencing my critique (although there will be some of that here as well), is to consider what cultural studies has achieved. As a named academic field it has been around for more than 40 years. It has been taught, more or less as a discipline, in universities in the UK and in Australia since at least the mid-1970s and early 1980s. It was slower to start up in Canada while, in the USA, the boom years were the 1990s – although one could argue that it has maintained its presence, if a little more modestly, into the 2000s. Other locations, and there are very many of them now, have their own starting points and narratives of development. For those of us who belong to the first generation of cultural studies scholars, baby-boomers most of us, cultural studies simply did not exist when we entered the university. Our training was in other, more traditional or established, disciplines – most often in English or sociology – and many of us have stories about our experience of those disciplines that explain what we sought to find in cultural studies. Now, some of us are professors of cultural studies and, whether we like it or not, pillars of the university community. Although it has had more than its share of detractors, critics and sceptics[1], cultural studies is recognized as a legitimate field of teaching and research in most places around the globe: by universities, national and international research funding bodies, publishers, booksellers, and even the occasional newspaper columnist. That is quite a transformation to have occurred within the careers of one generation – and in an institutional context which is not known for accommodating rapid change. Something has certainly happened – and so there are major achievements to be acknowledged.

This chapter will therefore engage in a (very) selective stock-take of what I think we might claim so far as among the achievements of cultural studies. For a start, I hope that it is uncontroversial to suggest that cultural studies has helped to place the construction of everyday life at the centre of contemporary intellectual enquiry and research in the humanities[2]. Along the way, it has played its part in opening up a number of cognate disciplines – literary studies, history, cultural geography, film and media studies, cultural anthropology, and even sociology – to analytic approaches and theoretical perspectives that have proved significant in their impact. Most particularly, cultural studies enabled the study of the media to be developed in ways that broke significantly with previous approaches by establishing new kinds of critical analytic practice. In general, I am prepared to defend the claim that the landscape of the humanities and the social sciences has been transformed by cultural studies over the past 30 years. I would also be happy to argue that the landscape of public debate has changed significantly as we have witnessed the penetration of cultural studies approaches, discourses and knowledges into public discourse to an extent that exceeds all expectations. It is easy (indeed, common) to overlook this dimension of cultural studies' impact. I am reminded of David Morley's citation of a book reviewer's comment that cultural studies was no more than a series of 'truisms', and 'so obviously a move in the direction of common sense that it hardly deserves all this attention'. Morley's response – a response that was right on the money in my view – was to point out that 'if the things that this reviewer refers to are now "common sense" they are largely so because work in cultural studies has made them so' (1998: 477).

There is no doubt that cultural studies' achievements are subject to vigorous internal and external debate – its internationalization, for instance, is still not universally regarded as a good thing (I argue at some length in Chapter 5, drawing on the example of the Inter-Asia Cultural Studies movement, that it is among cultural studies' genuine accomplishments). There is also debate about cultural studies' increasing integration with more established disciplines and networks; the fear is that this weakens cultural studies' critical capacity and its foundational challenge to disciplinarity. For some, what amounts to the re-incorporation of cultural studies into the academy may reflect a diminution of its critical project, and thus the beginning of an entropic cycle for the field as a whole. For others, since cultural studies has accomplished the disciplinary corrections it was set up to produce, and since it has neither the aspirations nor the epistemological equipment to become a discipline itself, cultural studies is now effectively over. Finally, there is (always!) debate about how relevant or important the 'project' of cultural studies has remained: its theoretical interest in the analysis of the cultural production and distribution of power, the critical dimension of its practice – and also perhaps the romanticism of its characteristic claim to intervene in the political processes it sets out to examine (Grossberg, 2010: 96–7). In the following chapters, these debates and issues will continue to run under the surface of my account of what has become of cultural studies.

THE INSTITUTION OF CULTURAL STUDIES

This subheading is a provocative one in this context, perhaps, but it does seem to me that the first thing I need to do is to point to cultural studies' remarkable success at creating space for itself within the university, as well as within other institutional contexts – research funding bodies, for instance – around the world. In at least one case of which I am aware, Lingnan University in Hong Kong, where the 2010 Crossroads conference was held (as we shall see in a later chapter, a very different event from that held in Birmingham!), cultural studies is officially represented as one of the flagship programmes for the whole university. While such institutional success will always be the result of concerted political effort, it is an effort that for much of the history of cultural studies has been disavowed. Readers may remember a special issue of *Cultural Studies* from 1998, edited by Ted Striphas and dedicated to discussing what was at the time deemed to be the 'problem' of the institutionalization of cultural studies. That such a topic was considered to be important reflects the fact that, from its beginning, cultural studies had maintained a principled objection to its own institutionalization. While it certainly sought recognition and respect, it also saw itself as opposed to the disciplinary formations that organized the university and warned against aligning the development of cultural studies' teaching programmes and research agendas too closely with the interests of the institution in which these activities took place. Such an accommodation, it was argued, ran against the grain of cultural studies' critical project. As cultural studies began to expand and internationalize – finding varied ways to establish itself in university systems around the world – many in cultural studies recognized that it was going to be increasingly difficult to maintain such a position[3]. Ted Striphas, in his introduction to the special issue, both reported and challenged the orthodoxies informing this stance:

> cultural studies has developed something of a 'line', so to speak, in response to the 'question' of institutionalization – despite its professed

disdain for ready-made answers. When the prospect of institutionaliz-
ing cultural studies gets posed, published reactions often tend towards
some variation of 'Resist disciplinarity!' I wonder, however, how productive this response is, given the practical and historical exigencies
facing cultural studies, particularly as it finds itself increasingly institutionalized. (1998: 459)

Striphas' strategy for challenging this orthodoxy was to frame his
approach around how, 'practically speaking', cultural studies
practitioners have *actually* dealt with 'negotiating the institu-
tional/disciplinary space'. His introduction is sceptical about the
reality ('practically speaking') of the orthodox position; he
politely submits that 'the polemical announcement of cultural
studies' 'anti-disciplinarity' seems to lack 'a discrete or recogniz-
able institutional embodiment' (480). That is, to put it more
bluntly, all the talk about anti-disciplinarity and resistance to the
institution loses much of its credibility when we notice that most
of it comes from those who have tenured positions teaching cultural studies as a named disciplinary formation through established programmes within the university system. As Tony Bennett,
one of the contributors to the special issue, points out: '[if] we
survey the scene today, cultural studies has all the institutional
trappings of a discipline' (1998: 530). To deny this would be
disingenuous, Bennett suggests, rewriting a history in which the
development of cultural studies has in fact always 'depended on
definite institutional conditions'. Importantly, he goes on, 'the
fact that these do not happen to be entirely the same as those
which have sustained the development of other disciplines is ...
no reason to characterize them as extra-institutional' (534).

   These days, perhaps, many would admit that this resistance to
disciplinarity has become more of a fashionable fiction than an
actual practice (Chapter 2 takes up this issue), but it was still a
question for serious debate at the time Striphas's issue was published – and, indeed, it had taken on added urgency as a direct
result of cultural studies' increasing penetration into the American
university system. Striphas is quite brave in confronting the issue

head-on: he uses the second half of his introductory paper to defend the pragmatics of institutionalization, and to outline some ways in which this might be accomplished without abandoning the original objectives of the cultural studies project. Along the way, he astutely points out how mistaken it would be to assume any neat homology between interdisciplinarity (or anti-disciplinarity) and a resistance to institutionalization. Indeed, Striphas notes how handy it has been for the corporatizing university, seeking economies of scale and financial efficiencies as well as a competitive position in the market, to make use of interdisciplinarity as an academic rationale for the administrative merging of disciplines, departments or schools. As he sees it, in this context, cultural studies' preferred institutional practices run the risk of unwittingly 'colluding with the university's corporatist logic (of which interdisciplinarity often – and ironically – is a symptom)' (1998: 454). This is one of the earlier warnings about what has in fact turned out to be a significant factor in cultural studies' institutionalization over the last decade. Despite its principled opposition to institutionalization and the corporate university, I think it is possible to see cultural studies as among the unlikely beneficiaries of the neo-liberal attack on the humanities in higher education. While I am not suggesting that such an outcome was something anyone in our field set out to achieve, nonetheless, the fact is that it would be rare these days to find a humanities administrative unit in any university that is not embedded within some kind of multidisciplinary formation. Such a formation might well be the product of a legitimate arrangement of cognate disciplines but it is also just as likely to be the outcome of a cynically arranged shotgun wedding between the academic administrative units concerned. All too often, cultural studies is used as the legitimating, interdisciplinary glue which holds such unions together and, as such, has made itself useful if not indispensable to the whole enterprise.

Even though the 1990s debates about institutionalization still linger somewhere or other, and can still surprise us by resurfacing with renewed intensity from time to time, on the whole it has to be admitted that talk about cultural studies resisting institution-alization today just sounds like a fantasy. Indeed, if we examined the past decade, it would be much easier to find examples of cultural studies' outstanding success at institutionalization than to find examples of heroic resistance to it. Undergraduate teaching programmes abound, postgraduate students do too; cultural studies research centres have proliferated and prospered; cultural studies academics find themselves on national academic committees, research funding assessment panels, government advisory boards, and in the media. In the most sincere form of flattery, some of our colleagues in other disciplines even find it politic (from time to time) to occasionally pretend to be one of us (I am thinking of the number of research grant applications I see these days, especially from literary studies, which self-nominate as cultural studies in the curious hope of enhancing their chances of success). Even though there are certain places, such as in the UK daily press (most egregiously, in left-leaning 'quality' papers such as *The Guardian*), where cultural studies is routinely parodied and its legitimacy questioned, I think it is defensible to regard this, by and large, as a marker of cultural studies' success rather than its vulnerability.

However, that is not all one would want to say about this. Indeed, in a controversial 2009 article published in the *Chronicle of Higher Education*, called 'What's the matter with cultural studies?', Michael Bérubé offers a very different assessment of the institutionalization of cultural studies today:

> *Policing the Crisis: Mugging, the State and Law and Order* (1978), the Birmingham collection that predicted the British Labour Party's epochal demise, is now more than 30 years old. In that time, has cultural studies transformed the disciplines of the human sciences? Has cultural studies changed the means of transmission of knowledge? Has cultural studies made the American university a more egalitarian or progressive institution? Those seem to me to be useful questions to ask, and one useful way of answering them is to say, sadly, no. Cultural studies hasn't had much of an impact at all. (2009: 1)

While Bérubé acknowledges there are some 'worthy programs in cultural studies at some North American universities, like Kansas State and George Mason, where there were once no programs at all' (1), nonetheless he regards this as a disappointingly modest achievement. I am aware that many of Bérubé's colleagues in cultural studies in the USA were profoundly dismayed by the publication of this piece; the message it sent to deans looking for programmes to cut can't have been helpful. If we set aside the politics of his intervention for the moment, however, he does have a point. One remembers the high hopes of those introducing cultural studies to America in the early 1990s[4], as well as the level of hyperbole that surrounded this venture. At the 1990s 'Cultural Studies Now and in the Future' conference at Champaign–Urbana, which is so often regarded as the moment when the cultural studies invasion of America was launched, Stuart Hall addressed concerns raised by what he described as 'the enormous explosion of cultural studies in the US, its rapid professionalization and institutionalization' (1992: 285). A decade later, in their introduction to a volume which constructs an extremely interesting version of 'American cultural studies', Hartley and Pearson (2000) refer to the institutionalization of cultural studies in the USA, as if it had proven to be a more widespread phenomenon there even than its British counterpart had been in the UK; they refer, further, to cultural studies 'installation in American universities as a mainstream subject for undergraduate and graduate study' (10). Given the fact that there were, even at the peak of this invasion, only a tiny handful of undergraduate programmes to name themselves as cultural studies (the effect was primarily on graduate programmes), such comments offer us an insight into what had become more like a reflection of the *zeitgeist* that had been whipped up around cultural studies in the 1990s rather than an accurate account of what was actually going on in the universities. Given such hyperbole, it is certainly understandable that Bérubé should regard what has become of this movement as a depressingly modest result.

It is, of course, remarkable when one considers how structurally important America has become to the international institutionalization of cultural studies (the proportion of international journals located there, the number of American scholars who identify with the field, and, most importantly, the crucial role played by the American market for our books), that the cultural studies' institutional presence in the American university system has remained so limited. Bérubé goes on:

> In most universities, cultural studies has no home at all, which means (among other things) that graduate students doing work in cultural studies have to hope they'll be hired in some congenial department that has a cultural studies component. The good news on that front is that you can now find cultural-studies scholars working in anthropology, in critical geography, even in kinesiology. In 'museum studies' and cultural ethnography, in the work of Mike Davis and Edward W. Soja on cities, and in analyses of West African soccer clubs or the career of Tiger Woods, cultural studies has cast a wide net. The bad news is that the place where cultural studies has arguably had the greatest impact is in English departments. And though people in English departments habitually forget this, English departments are just a tiny part of the university. (2009: 2)

On the one hand, from what I can tell from my own experience of the USA, this looks like an accurate characterization (even though some respondents to Bérubé's piece described it as a 'Jeremaid')[5]. On the other hand, this situation may well be the predictable consequence of what might now be seen as the unrealistic ambitions that accompanied the development of cultural studies in the USA over the 1990s. Given what is still a relatively traditional, discipline-bound structure for so much of the American higher education system, it is not surprising that American undergraduate programmes have not been quite as eager to take up the interdisciplinary ventures from the 'new humanities' as have their counterparts in the UK and Australia, for instance – and this affects more than just cultural studies.

More positively, it could also be the case that the relative stability of that traditional disciplinary structure probably influenced how easily the established disciplines could afford to absorb, accept or appropriate selected examples of the work coming from cultural studies, gender studies and the like. Furthermore, the distance between the American academy and the coalface of politics always meant that even a highly successful American cultural studies would never have the socio-political purchase that cultural studies has come to enjoy in Britain or Australia. Nonetheless, among the more curious aspects of the international formation of cultural studies – and it is hard to get a reliable figure on this – is the fact that there can't be more than about 20 graduate programmes in the USA at present which use the name 'cultural studies' in their title[6]. There are even fewer undergraduate degrees available in the USA with that nomenclature. This, in a system of more than 2,000 universities. As we go through this book we will repeatedly encounter the paradox that even though the US book market is crucial to cultural studies' commercial success as a publishing category, and even though US universities have provided comfortable homes for many international cultural studies scholars, it has not been the location for cultural studies' most significant institutional success. As Bérubé (2009) says, it is only a tiny presence in undergraduate teaching programmes, it has to fight for space in interdisciplinary initiatives at the graduate level, and it has no presence at all in the school curricula.

You get a very different picture elsewhere; there are certainly many more programmes, proportionally, in the UK, Australia, Canada, Hong Kong and Taiwan, which use the name of cultural studies and which situate themselves explicitly within the field. In the UK, in a system of around 140 universities, by my rough count, there about 10 schools or departments which name themselves as cultural studies, at least 17 undergraduate programmes and 14 graduate programmes. In addition, of course, there would be much cultural studies teaching going on under other names – in departments of English, media studies, communications and so on. Around the world, there are also numerous research centres devoted to cultural studies research – most notably in the UK but elsewhere as well. Indeed, in Australia, it is the cultural studies research centres such as the Centre for Cultural Research founded by Ien Ang at the University of Western Sydney (and less modestly, the Centre for Critical and Cultural Studies at the University of Queensland) that have been among the most successful humanities research initiatives in recent years. In the UK, Australia and Hong Kong, the influence of cultural studies on secondary school curricula has been substantial.

It is possible, then, to develop an institutional history of cultural studies that would provide us with evidence of its achievements and of its capacity to create an acknowledged space for its knowledges in various contexts. There are limits to what this history can legitimately tell us about 'cultural studies', though. It is important to recognize that the institutional histories of cultural studies in the various places it has been established are highly contingent upon the regulatory, political, disciplinary and funding frameworks in place there at the time. To see these histories as in some fundamental, organic, manner emerging from the thing that is cultural studies itself, therefore strikes me as a mistake. In this respect, then, and notwithstanding the long genealogy of debates within cultural studies about its institutionalization, it is inaccurate and unhelpful to think of cultural studies as an institution that operates across national boundaries and jurisdictions in a uniform or consistent manner. So what I want to do now is to talk about cultural studies in what is a slightly more comfortable or consistent formation, as a field of academic practice. I want to consider what cultural studies, thought of in this way, has achieved in terms of influencing or enabling new kinds of work across the humanities.

CULTURAL STUDIES AND ...

We are now in the era of the edited 'handbook' – big, compendious beasts aimed at a market seeking something between a work of reference and a textbook and comprised of either many short, encyclopaedic entries or long, authoritative but synoptic, essays on key aspects of the field in question. As someone who has written textbooks in a number of areas, I find that I am sometimes among those invited to write for these handbooks. Occasionally these invitations concern cultural studies alone, but more often they are about cultural studies and something else – cultural studies and film studies, or media and communications studies, or television studies. In such cases, the editors are usually interested in my discussing how cultural studies has changed the other field of study. At times there is a very specific story to tell – as in the case of film studies, for instance, as we shall see shortly; in other cases, such as television studies, in my view it can be quite difficult to distinguish the distinctive contribution made by cultural studies because the two disciplines have become so thoroughly intertwined (which, of course, could itself be seen as evidence of cultural studies' influence). The point I want to make from this, though, is that this does seem to me to provide clear, if anecdotal, evidence that Bérubé's assessment of cultural studies' impact on the human sciences might be challenged once we move beyond the institutional context and consider instead cultural studies' activity in the free trade of ideas. It has become widely acknowledged, I would suggest, that cultural studies has not only performed its by now notorious role of raiding other disciplines for bits and pieces of their methodologies, but that it has also operated as a contributor to, indeed in some cases an enabler of, the development or renovation of other disciplines.

These activities have been of a varied kind. I don't want to go over the territory explored in the fifth chapter of my *British Cultural Studies: An Introduction* (2003), which traces cultural studies' relations with history, sociology, and a number of other disciplines or fields. Interested readers can follow this up for themselves. Rather, I want to highlight several instances that can serve as examples of the particular kinds of influence I want to suggest that cultural studies has generated. In my first example, film studies, what cultural studies can claim to have done is to significantly extend the purchase of film studies by showing how it might approach new objects of study, new contexts of consumption, and alternative ways of thinking about how film texts generate both their pleasures and their meanings.

I should admit that I can't claim to be a disinterested observer here. My film studies textbook *Film as Social Practice* (the first edition of which was published in1988), was explicitly designed as a cultural studies perspective on the study of film. It broke with the aesthetic or predominantly textual modes of analysis that prevailed at the time in order to situate film as a social, rather than only a textual, practice within popular culture. Then, my *The Film Cultures Reader* (2002) highlighted recent directions in the study of film as culture, as industry, or as social practice and included among these directions the influence of cultural studies and cultural history on the methodologies used to study film and popular culture. As I point out elsewhere (Turner, 2008a: 270–1), any demonstration of this influence needs to acknowledge the very different histories of this relationship in, say, the UK or the USA – and the very different formations of both cultural studies and film studies in the varied locations in which they occur. Nonetheless, the story is worth retelling.

When cultural studies began in the USA, it was not much interested in film. That disinterest was at first enthusiastically reciprocated by a film studies that was dominated by an aesthetic and canonical approach to film texts, which was well established as a discrete disciplinary formation, and thus was in little need of constructing alliances with the likes of cultural studies. In the UK, I have suggested, it was very different:

Film Studies took longer to establish itself in the university system, and when it did gain a foothold there, film theory and cultural studies developed more or less in tandem. During the 1970s and the 1980s, proponents of both traditions participated enthusiastically in many of the same debates – albeit often from competing points of view. In the late 1970s, for instance, the Birmingham

Centre for Contemporary Cultural Studies devoted a whole research project to debating and refining the textual approaches identified with the editorial position articulated in the pages of the journal, *Screen* (for example, see Hall 1980; Morley, 1980). The popular success and broadly cross-disciplinary application of an early outcome of such debates, John Berger's *Ways of Seeing* (1972), indicates something of the contemporary consensus around the problems to be addressed – and the methodologies available – within cultural, representational, and film theory at that time. (Turner, 2008a: 271)

As the shared interest in understanding the text/spectator/audience relation lost its prominence for cultural studies in the early 1990s, the trajectories of the two fields began to describe different paths. However, the intellectual trade between the two fields continued and, as we shall see, it is probably not controversial to suggest that the British version of film studies has, progressively, taken on a character that owes a significant debt to its connection with work in cultural studies.

In my view, that is all to the good. There are certainly specific areas of film studies which were poorly developed, if not simply ignored, until cultural studies work started to be picked up by film scholars. The 1970s version of film studies – wherever we might want to locate it – was not well equipped to deal with popular cinema, with films that aimed at being entertainments rather than high art. At that time, film studies did not have a developed theory of the popular, and it was to remain untouched for many years by the increasing sophistication of television studies' analyses of the audience, or by cultural studies' broader understandings of media consumption. Film theory's single-minded focus on the text and the 'spectator' meant that it neglected other aspects of the experience of cinema-going – especially those which connected it to the practices of film culture that were more social than aesthetic. Finally, as new technologies emerged and as film culture gave way to screen cultures, it became even less tenable to focus so exclusively upon theories of representation.

British television studies – itself at this point a major focus for cultural studies – needs to be recognized as a serious interlocutor for British film studies as early as the mid-1980s (Kuhn, 1984). Given the strength of British television studies over the 1980s, and given the lack of any particularly strong boundaries between the fields – with scholars moving between them without any indication of breaching a border – it is probably not surprising that the connection between film and television studies resulted in British film studies' transformation over the 1980s and 1990s. By 2000, Gledhill and Williams were telling us we had to 'reinvent' film studies in ways that accommodate the shift towards dealing with popular film genres, film audiences and the social context of film texts, their production and consumption – all employing perspectives that had been shaped by cultural studies. I would regard the work of Yvonne Tasker (1993) on popular action cinema, for example, as representative of such a shift. A broader interest in film as the focal point of a larger set of socio-cultural relations is also evident in Jackie Stacey's study of film audiences, *Star Gazing* (1993). I have characterized this shift as one that takes British film studies from analysing film as an aesthetic object or as representation, towards understanding film as a social practice (Turner, 2008a).

In the USA, the shifts occur slightly later, but they did happen there as well. By the early 1990s, several important US film scholars were explicitly discussing the usefulness of British approaches to popular cinema and its audience. In particular, they drew on Bennett and Woollacott's (1987) study of the reception of the James Bond movies in which the notion of the 'reading formation' – a thoroughly cultural studies contextualization of reception – was outlined. Among the significant contributions to American film studies which make direct use of this work are Janet Staiger's *Interpreting Films* (1992) and *Perverse Spectators* (2000), as well as Barbara Klinger's *Melodrama and Meaning* (1994). More recently, the return of something like a new 'cinema of attractions' (Campora, 2009; Gunning, 1986) through new digital technologies, computer-generated imagery, and the rise of a cinema of special effects that privileges spectacle over narrative, has challenged film studies to further renovate its understandings of the cultural and technological contexts for both production and consumption.

To widen the frame now, it would not be an exaggeration to claim that film studies, by and large and wherever it is now practised, has experienced something of a 'cultural turn' as it has sought new explanations of the medium's function for its audiences. It is not alone there, of course, and perhaps this might suggest that the influence of cultural studies on the humanities disciplines has been relatively generalized. In my view, however, there are several areas where the influence of cultural studies on film studies has been direct, specific and generative, encouraging the development of a more diverse and pluralistic set of approaches for the discipline. Film studies got what it needed from cultural studies; and it could have got this from nowhere else. What it needed was indeed among the core contributions that cultural studies has made to the new humanities: its theorization of the popular, its interest in the pleasures of consumption and the experience of audiences, its openness to the meaningfulness of the practices of everyday life, and its determinedly contextualized account of representation. The result was a significant expansion of the discipline's purchase and an enhancement of the density of texture in its conceptual frameworks.

My second example highlights a perhaps even more fundamentally enabling contribution that cultural studies has made to the development of the many 'new humanities' interdisciplinary fields that have opened up in the past 20 or 30 years. Cultural studies' extensive theoretical literature has proven particularly helpful as a means of facilitating the intellectual trade across disciplines that shared an interest in the problematic of culture: that is, it provided some methodological strategies, as well as the theoretical rationale, to develop interdisciplinary fields through the mobilization of its conceptualization of culture and its application to particular research sites or problems. (I will return to this in the discussion of internationalization in

Chapter 5.) One of the more explicit examples, where the field in question spent a great deal of time discussing its relation with cultural studies, is American studies.

Over the 1970s and 1980s, a particularly common and fruitful mode of multidisciplinary study was in many places called area studies – Latin American studies, Australian studies, American studies and so on. Most of these programmes – and I graduated from one myself in the late 1970s, the English and American studies programme at the University of East Anglia (UEA) – were in fact loosely structured multidisciplinary programmes in which students could study their 'area' (that is, say, America or Australia) from a number of disciplinary perspectives (at UEA, when I was there, the dominant disciplines were literary studies, history and cinema studies). Often there was discussion about the theoretical resources available to make an area study more properly interdisciplinary as distinct from multidisciplinary[7]: that is, to find a way to connect the outcomes of the individual disciplines' enquiries through a set of analytic or explanatory protocols that would provide the area with something like a methodology or a core theoretical framework. As the contributing disciplines responded to the waves of theoretical development that began hitting them from the early 1970s onwards, and as the tide of European cultural and literary theory rose, there was increasing pressure to find a way to endow area studies with an equivalent level of theoretical sophistication. Cultural studies in Australia, for instance, harangued Australian studies for its lack of 'theory' and staged a short-lived campaign to renovate it or perhaps to incorporate it – in the end, to no avail[8]: ultimately, the two fields went their own ways and a tradition that would go on to describe itself informally as Australian cultural studies was the result.

It was different for American studies. From the 1970s onward into the 2000s, American studies has been engaged in a wide-ranging debate about the nature and future of the field: as the so-called 'myth and symbol' paradigm was losing its dominance, as new social and political formations demanded to be reflected in the questions asked by American studies scholars, and as the commitment to 'American exceptionalism'[9] was questioned. Among these debates, particularly as we head into the 1980s and 1990s, there was a discussion about the usefulness of an upstart British cultural studies in helping American studies deal with what had long been criticized as its failure to 'critically and systematically analyze concepts of culture' (Sklar, 1975: 260). From the outside, it seems as if these discussions generated plenty of heat: George Lipsitz dramatizes this by his ironic proclamation that 'a specter is haunting American Studies, the specter of European cultural theory':

> During the past two decades, European critics from a variety of perspectives have theorized a 'crisis of representation' that has called into question basic assumptions within the disciplines central to the American Studies project – literary studies, art history, anthropology, geography, history and legal studies. From the structuralist Marxism of Louis Althusser to the psychoanalytic interventions of Jaques Lacan, from Foucauldian post-structuralism to the French feminism of Luce Irigaray and Hélène Cixous, from Derridean deconstruction to the dialogic criticism of Mikhail Bakhtin, European theory has revolutionized the study of culture. (1990: 616)

Lipsitz' response to this revolution is to embrace it, highlighting the homology between the politics underpinning so much of European cultural theory[10] with the politics informing the beginnings of American studies in the 1930s, as well as the 'affinity between European cultural theory and American popular culture' that makes cultural studies seem a comfortable fit[11] with American studies:

> ... [C]ontemporary European cultural theory resonates with the categories and questions of American Studies traditions: indeed, it is fair to say that the development of American Studies itself anticipated many of the cross-disciplinary epistemological and hermeneutic concerns at the heart of European cultural theory (622).

Even though parts of the history of American Studies were pre-occupied with what Lipsitz describes as a 'mythical cultural consensus', he argues that this 'did not prevent American Studies scholars from asking critical questions about the relationship between the social construction of cultural categories and power relations in American society' (622). Given that the focus of American studies was upon culture, and given the lack of any American equivalent to the strong ideological impediment to the focus upon popular culture and everyday life experienced in the UK (I am thinking of what is usually called the 'culture and civilization tradition' (see Turner, 2003: 34–8)), there were good reasons why American studies, as it reconsidered what it should do and for whom, might turn to cultural studies. That is certainly how some of cultural studies' advocates within American studies put it; as Barry Shanks described the situation in 1997, cultural studies 'provided compelling new answers to the most central problem that had haunted the field: how is "culture" itself best understood and best investigated?' (1997: 96–7). British cultural studies, Shanks goes on to say, may not have solved this problem for all American studies scholars but it did provide 'new ways to work and think productively within the tensions they described' (97). Importantly, and this is a dimension of the early work in cultural studies that tends to be forgotten these days, Shanks points out that British cultural studies provided a demonstration of how cultural theory could be integrated into, and inform, empirical work . 'Throughout the eighties', Shanks reminds us, 'even as theoretical exploration of cultural processes grew ever more elaborate (and, yes, perhaps arcane), British cultural studies never lost its focus on empirical research in concrete situations'(109), and it demonstrated how these two activities could proceed in a productive partnership.

Most would see American studies as having been transformed over this period, and when you look at subsequent edited collections and anthologies (for example Radway et al., 2009), their task seems to be one of processing that transformation, reporting and explaining it to a still heterogeneous and dynamic constituency of

American studies scholars. Hartley and Pearson, in particular, construct an ingenious blend of American studies and cultural studies to produce the 'American Cultural Studies' of their anthology, that recognizes the part played by both intellectual traditions – the provincial or national tradition of American studies, and the imported and then indigenized contributions from British cultural studies (2000). It is not controversial to argue that, within the practice of American studies in the 1990s and into the 2000s, cultural studies played a significant and perhaps even at times a dominant role in terms of shifting the kinds of subject matter and topics approached within the field (more work on media, popular culture, and everyday life, in the first instance) as well as the theoretical perspectives adopted. The debates did not terminate there, however, and American studies has continued to be a lively, dynamic and highly contested field in which the politics of academic practice has been at the forefront now for quite some time. The media and popular culture end of cultural studies is not so prominent today, I am told by those working in the field, and theoretically inflected modes of cultural history seem to be filling that gap.

I do not claim any recent expertise in American studies, so this is very much an outsider's account; within the field, I am sure there are nuances and complexities I have overlooked. Nonetheless, the point I am making here is not just that cultural studies played an important role in the ongoing transformation of American studies, but that what cultural studies has been able to do – in area studies and elsewhere – is to provide an example of how one might deal with the problematic of culture within an interdisciplinary field. Culture, as imported from cultural studies, was then an enabling concept – not so much because it came with prescribed methods, but because it was already a well-developed (but not settled) focus for further debate, elaboration, analysis and application. Typically, where area studies had maintained their parallel disciplinary models but had largely relied on their juxtaposition as a means of seeking some interdisciplinary exchange, what cultural studies directly addressed and indeed enabled was the *articulation*[12] of these models and their perspectives. While some area studies and interdisciplinary fields sought out other avenues, it is clear that for many in American studies, as well as in gender studies, sexuality studies and a range of other 'new humanities' fields, cultural studies' capacity to theorize the processes of articulation was a fundamental benefit.

CONCLUSION

I want to conclude this chapter by returning to the question asked by Michael Bérubé (2009): how have university studies in the humanities changed as a result of cultural studies? That seems to me a thoroughly legitimate question to ask and I want to provide a response.

Now, the first, and to my mind the really obvious, answer to this is that cultural studies rescued the media, contemporary popular culture and everyday life from the neglect (or, worse, from the distaste) of the traditional or established disciplines. I know, of course, that many scholars from these other disciplines – particularly from sociology, anthropology and English – angrily refute this, and indeed regard cultural studies as having appropriated *their* subject areas. I am not going to rehearse what are now very familiar and probably permanently unresolved debates in order to start arguing about this all over again. I am sure most of us long ago lost patience with this dispute. But, for the record, let me simply state that, like just about everybody else in cultural studies, I reject such claims. Certainly cultural studies shared with a discipline such as sociology an interest in some of the same social phenomena, but what has always marked the difference between these two intellectual traditions is cultural studies' theoretical engagement with representation and a commitment to the social and political usefulness of the products of that engagement[13]. Hence, cultural studies' early and distinctive focus on theorizing the text (and, conversely, the empirical disciplines' disparagement of this work), as well as its application of such theories to the analysis of the contemporary media. However, the crucial point I would want to stress is that, yes, there certainly *are* disciplines which could have seen the things that were done later by cultural studies as among their legitimate objects of enquiry. Largely, however, they ignored them because they did not recognize their importance – until, that is, they were developed as the objects of cultural studies. My characterization of how the established disciplines dealt with the media and popular culture before cultural studies turned up compares their treatment to that of an old car that someone had abandoned to rust in a vacant lot. It was cultural studies that hopped in, hot-wired it and drove it away, took it to the body shop to be repaired and customized, only to find that when they took it out for a spin the previous owners chased them down the road, yelling out 'Hey, that's my car!'

My second answer to the question is that cultural studies, in its various formations and influences, has played a part in renovating, recharging or otherwise transforming what gets done in particular disciplines. Again, there is a reasonably extensive literature on this – particularly the relations between cultural studies and history, or cultural geography, or literary studies[14]. By way of providing a further example, a less widely circulated story can be told about cultural studies' influence on the field of Asian studies in Australia. Asian studies does have a long history there and therefore almost inevitably has retained elements of a residually Orientalist academic practice: even now it still has one or two 'old China hands' who maintain an elitist, conservative or traditional view of what constitutes an appropriate research topic – let alone what constitutes an appropriate research method. While Asian studies is plural, the established paradigm for most of the older generation of Asian studies scholars was that they pursued an interest in one particular country rather than a region and, in most cases, this was from a single, traditionally disciplinary, point of view. In the 1990s, as some younger Asian studies scholars with backgrounds in media studies, cultural studies or literary theory began to take up topics to do with the media, popular culture or the politics of representation around sexuality, gender and ethnicity[15], and to do so in ways that employed a more comparative research practice, a generational divide developed. While initially this division was policed, if not by blanket exclusion then certainly by the open disparagement of such work within the Asian studies community, cultural studies (and not just in Australia) provided a congenial alternative context in which some of these scholars could publish or present their work. This enabled the coming generation of Asian studies scholars to do work that was dramatically different to that of their predecessors: explicitly theorized, interdisciplinary and comparative, focused largely around issues of representation and popular culture within Asia, their work has found itself uniquely placed to engage productively with the burst of cultural modernization that has transformed so many countries in the region. As international recognition grew, and as Australian cultural studies itself gained prominence and respectability, the new generation of Asian studies scholar was no longer so vulnerable to the disapproval of their colleagues. Today, this new wave of scholars is close to exercising a dominant influence on what constitutes Asian studies in Australia and is constructing closer collaborative ties with the well-established networks of cultural studies scholars within Asia itself. As a result, a field that was looking moribund a decade or so ago is now vibrant and expanding and increasingly transnational: its relations to other interdisciplinary fields – cultural studies, communications studies, gender studies and so on – are prospering, to the benefit of all.

There are many other things one might mention in response to Bérubé's question as a means of nominating what cultural studies can legitimately claim to have achieved. However, that is probably enough for the moment. The task for me now is to begin to focus on some aspects of the practice of cultural studies today, including some that were no doubt the provocation to the rhetorical question mentioned in the introduction – 'Is this what we have become?' It is time to move on to my analysis of some of the more worrying things cultural studies has become in order to outline my critique of the contemporary practice of cultural studies. When Stuart Hall is reported as saying that he cannot bear to read another analysis of *The Sopranos* (McCabe, 2007: 29), on the one hand, and when so many people are writing analyses of *The Sopranos*, on the other hand, the warning bells for cultural studies should be ringing. I am certainly hearing these warning bells loud and clear, and I want to devote the rest of the book to discussing what I think may have set them off.

NOTES

1   Among my favourite examples of the rancorous dismissal of cultural studies is Bourdieu and Wacquant's thumbnail definition of the field: 'Cultural Studies, this mongrel domain, born in England in the 1970s, which owes its international dissemination (which is the whole of its existence) to a successful publishing policy' (1999: 47).

2   Cultural studies is not alone in this, of course, but it has certainly played its part in contributing to what has become something of an ethnographic turn in the humanities and social sciences.

3   In Hall's 2007 interview with Colin McCabe, he acknowledges both of these points: 'the institutionalization was inevitable', he says. 'Cultural studies would have disappeared if it hadn't become institutionalised, but the process of institutionalization itself kind of robbed it of some of its cutting edge' (McCabe, 2007: 28).

4   The most significant monument to these, of course, is the Grossberg et al. (eds) (1992) *Cultural Studies* anthology taken from the presentations at the famous 'Cultural studies: Now and in the Future' conference at the University of Illinois, Champaign–Urbana, in 1990. This volume carried the promise of changing the face of the humanities and social sciences in America, and certainly achieved extraordinary prominence for some time. One of its most notable reviews was by Bérubé himself: it was featured on the cover of *The Village Voice* (Bérubé, 1992), and it compared the epochal significance of the arrival of cultural studies to the Beatles' first performance at Carnegie Hall.

5   It is also supported by the analysis presented in David Shumway's paper at the 2010 Crossroads conference in Hong Kong: 'When Institutions haven't been built: Cultural Studies in the US'.

6 In Gilbert Rodman's CULSTUDS list of cultural studies programmes, there are 16 listed which actually use the phrase cultural studies in their title (http://com.umn.edu/-grodman/cultstud/programs.html (last accessed 27 January 2010)); In Kansas State University's advice to its students on where they might enrol in a cultural studies graduate programme, 12 programmes are listed. Of these, only seven have the name cultural studies in the title of the school, department or programme (www.k-state.edu/english/programs/culturalstudies/phd.html (last accessed 27 January 2010)).

7 At its simplest, a multidisciplinary approach incorporates multiple disciplinary perspectives, independently and discretely applied, whereas an interdisciplinary approach involves a degree of mixing and collaboration between the disciplinary perspectives and thus a way of allowing them to 'talk' to each other. Typically, in the way it has been practised in the humanities, this tends to involve the one person working with the theoretical tools from more than one discipline.

8 See Turner (1996b).

9 An interesting place to read about these debates is Janice Radway's presidential address to the American Studies Association, 'What's in a name?' (1999).

10 Lipsitz is talking about more than cultural studies here: it is the whole enterprise that usually gets labelled Theory. However, it is clear that the cultural studies version of 'Theory' is the one that ends up being discussed at the greatest length in his essay, and it is largely the benefits of cultural studies approaches to which he points.

11 It is significant that during this period, Janice Radway, one of the major stars of American cultural studies after her book *Reading the Romance* (1984) was so widely taken up, was the president of the American Studies Association.

12 I am using this here in the specialized sense employed within British cultural studies; see, for instance, the short gloss in the introduction to Grossberg et al. (1992: 8), or for a more elaborated discussion see Jennifer Daryl Slack (1996).

13 An interesting discussion of the relations between sociology and cultural studies, written well before people's interest in this debate was exhausted, is Janet Wolff's 'Cultural studies and the sociology of culture' (1998).

14 I should point out that, in the case of literary studies, my sense is that this story does not necessarily have a happy ending. It may well be that what changed in literary studies was quite fundamental to its claims to

legitimacy. Sociologist Michèle Lamont makes an interesting observation in the context of her examination of the culture of research funding bodies in the humanities: that as literary studies broadened its disciplinary agenda towards cultural studies, and 'widened their interests to include history and anthropology', 'English scholars may have indirectly lowered the value of the purely literary analytical tools' (Lamont, 2009: 72) – that is, a particular form of close textual analysis. I think there is something to that, as well as to the notion that what the public values about literature is precisely the things that the academy now often disavows – the traditional canon, a notion of a universal aesthetics, and an ethical-moral reading of literary value. Despite the boom in literary theory that so dominated the 1980s and 1990s, my own observation is that in many places now literary studies is a discipline which has lost its coherence as a set of practices and is engaged on a new search for legitimacy.

15 Examples of this generation include Kam Louie's book on Chinese masculinity (2002), Vera Mackie's study of feminism in Japan (2003), and Antonia Kinnane's examinations of fashion in China (1999 with A. McLaren and 2007). There are clear continuities flowing from their more cultural studies inflected work to what I might describe more unequivocally as the 'cultural studies' generation, which includes scholars such as Stephanie Helmryk Donald, Mark McLelland, Larissa Hjorth, Audrey Yue and Fran Martin.

THE 'UNDISCIPLINE': CULTURAL STUDIES AND INTERDISCIPLINARITY

2

BEING 'UNDISCIPLINED'

In commencing this chapter by focusing on cultural studies' description of itself as the 'undiscipline', I acknowledge at the outset that this formulation is in some respects a straw man; it is true that this notion is far less current now than it once was. The reason why I am focusing on it, nonetheless, is that I am interested in what I perceive as its continuing influence on certain aspects of the practice of cultural studies, and in particular on how we approach the task of training our postgraduate students in *their* practice of cultural studies.

In what follows, I want to consider some of the limitations to the project of interdisciplinarity within which cultural studies locates itself. Much of what I have to say about the problems of maintaining and reproducing an interdisciplinary project applies to other interdisciplinary fields as well – gender studies or communications studies, for instance. These fields have also struggled with the same problems of finding ways to teach their students research methods that will generate continuity and rigour but without relinquishing the sense of intellectual openness and flexibility that is the clear benefit of an interdisciplinary project. In this respect, each field seems to have a particular problem that it must sort out before it can find a way of dealing with, but not rigidifying, its particular version of interdisciplinarity. Communications studies, for instance, especially in its heartland of the USA, continues to struggle with the management of the competing claims from its traditional disciplinary location in the quantitative social sciences, and the persistent but more recent claims from the critical and qualitative traditions represented by, for instance, cultural and media studies. Debates over the nomenclature for each of the divisions of the International Communications Association, for instance, continue to demonstrate the difficulty of maintaining a plausible balance between these two traditions, while also revealing that this is as much a political as an academic undertaking[1].

Among the things that are distinctive about the cultural studies version of an interdisciplinary project, however, is the explicitness with which it has outlined its objectives as both critical and political. It is not agnostic about what it studies, and has often announced that the end point of its practice is to understand and inform social and political change. Such a position challenges traditional notions of academic distance, and confronts longstanding conventions about how disinterested an academic discipline should be. Cultural studies has been unapologetic about this, and indeed has chosen to deal with criticism of its objectives through deliberate provocation: its refutation of the necessity of disciplinarity was, in part, a refusal of the conventions that would make its objectives inappropriate to an academic field.

As time has gone by that has become a much less provocative position to adopt, and its shock value has declined. It has remained on the books, though, and in my view the refusal of disciplinarity, which is what effectively I am referencing through the label of the 'undiscipline', constitutes a particular condition for the development and continuity of cultural studies – and a condition that continues to play a significant part in how cultural studies deals with the problem of sustaining an interdisciplinary project. Now, however, as we chart what has become of cultural studies, it is time to consider what I want to suggest are the negative consequences of this idea's residual presence in the contemporary practice of cultural studies.

The 'undiscipline' label was probably most widely circulated in the early 1990s, when it had become something of a routine formulation and was especially evident in the marketing and reviewing of the Grossberg et al. collection, *Cultural Studies* (1992). I should own up, though, that I am as guilty as anyone else of contributing to the mythologizing of this idea. Not only does it turn up, largely unchallenged, from time to time in my *British Cultural Studies: An Introduction* (1990, 1996a, 2003), but also in my *Nation, Culture, Text: Australian Cultural and Media Studies* (Turner, 1993a) that happily conformed with the orthodoxies of the times by concluding its introductory essay with a section entitled 'Undisciplines' which among other things noted that the 'virtue of being an "undiscipline" rather than an established discipline lies in cultural studies' provisionality and its emphasis on praxis', and stressed the importance of cultural studies remaining 'an undisciplined, contestatory, fluid field of theory and practice' (1993b: 12)[2]. I have a more complicated and nuanced view of this issue now. That said, and while I do consider that characterizing cultural studies as the undiscipline complacently romanticizes its engagement with interdisciplinarity, I do not want to underplay the fact that this engagement was crucial to the formation of cultural studies: through its principled and, for the time, pioneering commitment to the importance of the free play of intellectual inquiry across disciplinary boundaries. An interest in interdisciplinarity becomes more mainstream from the 1970s onwards, but the beginnings of cultural studies is one of the places where we can find criticism of the exclusionary practices of the traditional disciplines well before that time – in cultural studies, such criticism occurs early, it is applied consistently, and it is highly elaborated.

To provide a little context here, it is worth noting that liberal arts and humanities programmes in Western universities in the 1960s, when the Birmingham Centre for Contemporary Cultural Studies (CCCS) was established, were anything but playgrounds for the exercise of free choice. Typically, students were funnelled into one big survey course (in the British model, usually lasting a whole year) which introduced students to, and set the boundaries for, their discipline before presenting them with a short menu of choices for their senior years. An issue often discussed with students wishing eventually to pursue graduate study was the need to demonstrate 'coverage' through their choices from this menu – that is, the need to ensure that their choices covered all the important coordinates of the discipline rather than merely indulge their personal enthusiasms. Exercising free choice even within those offerings endorsed by the discipline was difficult enough; to move beyond these offerings and the research opportunities they circumscribed virtually impossible. Indeed, the disciplines' stranglehold over curricula generated some lively grassroots responses during the height of the international take-up of aspects of the Berkeley Free Speech Movement in the 1960s. There was a brief burst of interest in establishing 'Free Universities': informal and unaccredited counterculture alternatives to the official universities explicitly set up to challenge the disciplines' control over the content of undergraduate curricula. At Sydney University, when I was an undergraduate, university staff moonlighted at its Free University over a period of several years in order to teach, *pro bono*, subjects not sanctioned by their discipline but in demand by the students. Significantly, some of these subjects dealt with areas of popular culture such as popular music and they probably mark the earliest point at which teaching in any area of popular culture had occurred in Australia. In this context, then, the establishment of a graduate research programme that had the objective of subjecting popular culture to critical analysis from multidisciplinary perspectives might have been something that scholars dreamt of doing in the future; to actually carry it off in the present was quite an achievement.

Cultural studies became necessary, in a sense, as a means of formulating a coordinated intellectual response to the power of the traditional discipline and its tendency towards actively policing its borders. Operating as they did at this time, these disciplinary borders effectively excluded the core territory of cultural studies – the media, popular culture and everyday life. There is no doubt that the practitioners of cultural studies can legitimately claim a leading role among those to have mounted a significant and effective challenge to the power of the discipline.

Indeed, as cultural studies' history lengthens, the success of that original challenge has gradually obscured just how extraordinary an achievement it was. The subsequent normalization of interdisciplinary teaching and research within the Anglophone West makes it easy for us to forget this. Also in danger of being forgotten, as the postgraduates of today (understandably, perhaps) take these academic freedoms more or less for granted, is just how liberating it was to be relieved of one's oppressive subjection to the *discipline* of an academic field. It is possible these days to recover a sense of that release from the various interviews and memoirs written by those who were among the earliest cohorts of staff and students at the CCCS. It is there, for instance, in John Clarke's description, part of his account of cultural studies' introduction to America, a process that was in full swing at the time he was writing:

> The impact of being liberated from serving one's apprenticeship in an existing field formed part of the collective energy of the Centre (and may have contributed to the setting of somewhat grandiose thesis projects). This sense of liberation certainly helped to create a highly productive orientation towards established fields of knowledge. As outsiders, it was possible to approach them as objects of study (rather than as subjects to be absorbed), to raid them for useful knowledge, to criticize their limitations and to juxtapose them with other fields of knowledge to generate new insights and new directions. Relieved of disciplinary responsibility, the Centre aimed for knowledge without frontiers and pursued it across such boundaries with considerable self-confidence (or arrogance). (1991: 4)

Clarke helps us to understand why this freedom has been so highly valued since, and why it has continued to play a major role in the narratives of cultural studies as one of the most important capacities that the resistance to disciplinarity released.

Over time, however, the excitement Clarke describes has given way to a sense of entitlement – or perhaps to the view that the important battles have been won and that cultural studies scholars should be allowed to just get on with whatever it is they want to do without interference. Over this same period, as well, we have seen a steady increase in cultural studies academics' identification with modes of professionalization that are more comfortably aligned with the behaviours expected by their institutions. In this context, then, there is no longer much point to *actually* being undisciplined (although there is still some pleasure to be gained from thinking of oneself in that way).

The idea has also lost its cachet of exclusivity: cultural studies is far from the only field to have described itself as an undiscipline. As disciplinarity itself has become the bad object right across the new humanities, the label 'undiscipline' became the object of enthusiastic appropriation, particularly towards the end of the 1990s. Among the fields and disciplines which claimed the label around that time are American studies (Kilgore, 1997), the history of the book (!?) (Clegg, 2001), and anthropology (Thomas, 1999). As it became a little safer to do so, everyone was just dying to be undisciplined. These days, of course, mounting an attack on disciplinarity would be utterly redundant. In so many locations, university administrators have done that job for us – killing off the disciplinary department or school in order to remove them as obstacles to the mergers, restructures and administrative rearrangements that have been the preferred strategies of neoliberal higher education funding regimes. Indeed, my guess is that some of the folks who might once have taken up the cause of interdisciplinarity are now more likely to be locked in battles with their universities with the objective of securing their discipline's survival.

For these and other reasons I won't go into here, then, explicit arguments advocating opposition to disciplinarity have largely disappeared from the literature of cultural studies. What seems to have remained, though, is the implicit assumption that there is a contradiction between the cultural studies' project of interdisciplinary teaching and research on the one hand and cultural studies' thoroughgoing institutionalization as a *de facto* disciplinary formation on the other. As Striphas' special issue of *Cultural Studies* demonstrates, this formulation was still current at the end of the 1990s. However, as virtually all the contributors to that issue suggested, in one way or another, this was a position that needed to be jettisoned because it was simply no longer credible. This is even more the case today. While cultural studies has certainly maintained its commitment to interdisciplinarity consistently over its history, the time has long since passed when cultural studies might realistically contest the wisdom of allowing itself to become institutionalized as a discipline in its own right. In most places, effectively, that horse has already bolted. Nonetheless, in what follows, I want to argue that such a formulation continues to exert an influence on the practice of cultural studies today. That influence is visible in aspects of the design of many of our undergraduate teaching programmes, and in the ways many of us supervise and train our graduate students. It is the latter upon which I concentrate here; I discuss undergraduate teaching in the following chapter. In approaching this issue in this manner, I am conscious that there are a number of dimensions to disciplinarity: theoretical, methodological and pedagogic. While these categories will of course overlap in significant ways, my primary interest here and thus the focus of my discussion in this chapter is pedagogic[3].

THE LIMITS OF INTERDISCIPLINARITY

As I suggested earlier, cultural studies' foundational resistance to the power of the discipline constituted a significant and groundbreaking intervention into the established structures for university teaching and research in the UK. In the first instance, the specific intervention originated with those setting up the research programmes in Birmingham at the CCCS. Stuart Hall has pointed out that the CCCS was fortunate to have some 'cover' to protect it against repercussions from its unorthodox methods – the CCCS had an independent source of funds, it was led by the senior professor of English, and it had an allocated space within a well-established department of English.

Also, its activities were confined to the postgraduate population and were thus of less importance to the university at that time; indeed, Hall comments, perhaps underplaying the difficulties involved (although my own experience as a postgraduate student in the UK in the early 1970s would tend to support his view), that at the time 'postgraduate work was so poorly organized in Britain that you could do more or less what you wanted' (McCabe, 2007: 23). It is possible that the centre might have been allowed less rope if it had been dealing with undergraduates (which it eventually went on to do in the decade or so before it was closed down).

Even so, subsequent developments tell us that this intervention was groundbreaking only for a short period. Soon, everyone was doing it. Indeed, in a remarkably short space of time, not only the academic benefits, but also the rationalizing potential, of interdisciplinary approaches to institutional organization were embraced by those formulating higher education policies in a number of countries. By the early 1970s we are beginning to see whole universities – in Australia's case, a whole new tertiary sector – structured around the principle of interdisciplinarity. In the UK, new universities, in which the principle of academic organization was interdisciplinary from the start, were developed from the early 1960s (Sussex was the first, I believe, and it was established in 1961). In addition, the partnership between interdisciplinary curricula and a more pragmatic vocational mission for higher education was among the drivers of the development of the UK's polytechnics from the late 1970s. In Australia, the same connection was similarly embedded not only in the new universities established in the early 1970s (such as Griffith University in Brisbane and Murdoch University in Perth) but also in the establishment of a whole new higher education sector, the colleges of advanced education (CAEs)[4], which were set up to broaden public access to institutions that were 'equal but different' to the traditional universities due to their focus on interdisciplinary academic programsprogrammes with clear vocational outcomes (Turner, 1993b). Canada had its version of this, too, with the establishment of Trent University in 1964[5], for example, and the gradual transformation of the role and status of colleges such as Toronto's Ryerson over the next decade. Finally, while in the USA there was less institutional activity in terms of the establishment of interdisciplinary teaching programmes, as we saw in the previous chapter, it is interesting to note that the growth of university-based interdisciplinary humanities research centres and institutes takes off significantly over this period; examples include the Centre for Twentieth Century Studies at the University of Wisconsin–Milwaukee and the Humanities Centre at Stanford University. By 1988, there were enough of these institutions to justify the formation of a peak body to represent them, the international but US-based Consortium of Humanities Centres and Institutes (CHCI). Again, as we have seen in Chapter 1, this is also the time at which the debate about properly theorizing their practice of interdisciplinarity emerges in American studies.

All of this was a highly satisfying vindication of those who had advocated a more interdisciplinary approach to higher education, but one can't avoid noticing how well this mode of institutional organization aligned with the emerging needs of those responsible for administering university systems[6]. I am not suggesting that the embrace of a less traditional disciplinary structure was *not* driven, at least in part, by a genuine appreciation of how this might enliven the intellectual culture of the universities; nonetheless, it was certainly fortuitous that the new interdisciplinary administrative units enabled improved economies of scale, and facilitated the movement of money as well as ideas across disciplinary boundaries. This, in turn, improved the universities' cost structures during a period when there was a massive expansion in the demand for higher education. In the end, what brought benefits to the universities' bottom line also helped to create space for the interdisciplinary new humanities-gender studies, media studies, screen studies, and cultural studies. Consequently, it was in locations such as the new universities and the polytechnics in the UK, in the new interdisciplinary universities and the colleges of advanced education in Australia, and in Trent University in Canada slightly later on, where cultural studies had its early successes in establishing new undergraduate and, later on, graduate programmes.

In the light of this history, then, it is a bit of a stretch to continue advocating the homology that Striphas's introduction to his issue of *Cultural Studies* (1998) so rightly questioned: that is, the supposed link between cultural studies' principled support for interdisciplinarity and its equally principled opposition to institutionalization. Almost everywhere you look[7], the facts tell a different story. In general, and notwithstanding the inevitable variations from place to place, it is true to say that from the mid-1970s onwards a new breed of institutions dedicated to interdisciplinarity emerged in productive partnerships with precisely these new transdisciplinary theoretical formations in the humanities. Indeed, in my view, it is just this level of institutionalization which has facilitated these formations' attainment of a broader legitimacy within the university sector.

These developments were embraced at the time, of course, and interdisciplinarity has continued to be fundamental to the practice of cultural studies. The reasons for this are familiar: removing the boundaries between disciplines enables access to objects of study that are rendered invisible by the traditional disciplinary structures (and popular culture, of course, is a crucial example of that); the use of methods developed in other fields carries the potential of usefully de-contextualizing and de-familiarizing the objects or practices under examination, freeing them from the capture of one explanatory regime; porous disciplinary boundaries combat the tendency to colonize knowledge and organize it into self-contained fiefdoms that resist collaboration or cross-disciplinary fertilization; interdisciplinary fields have proven that they are able to respond more productively to the emergence of new theoretical problematics, such as culture or gender, that are not easily contained within any one of the existing disciplines; and they have fostered a more collaborative climate for the sharing, examination and possible application of theoretical or methodological advances made in other fields. Taken together, the development of these capacities has proven profoundly significant, transforming the academic landscape in the humanities over the past 50 years.

Notwithstanding all of this, I want to argue that there are some limitations to the usefulness or appropriateness of an interdisciplinary practice when it is employed as the only pedagogic approach to the teaching and training of the next generation of teachers and researchers for the field. In order to make this argument, I want to consider it from two perspectives: the first is through a discussion of the current practices and what they are producing for us at the moment, and the second is in relation to the long term prospects should these practices continue.

Focusing first on current practices, let's look at what I would suggest are now quite common approaches to the design of graduate course offerings[8]. Reviewing the offerings for postgraduates in cultural studies programmes from country to country reveals an extraordinary amount of diversity and (perhaps more accurately) contingency. Even though many of these graduates will be seeking employment in an international market and therefore must present themselves as generically equipped to teach cultural studies into all kinds of university programme, there is almost no such thing as a standard graduate course in the field. Institutional differences – often driven by the specifics of cultural studies' location in the organizational structure of each university – and differences in how programmes are situated and funded within different national systems will account for many of the variations. However, the mythology of the undiscipline plays its part as well. For a start, I suggest that it is implicated in the fact that there seems to be very little pressure on those preparing graduate students in cultural studies to design a teaching programme that presents an account of the field – as, in effect, a disciplinary formation. The reverse tends to happen. Licensed as they are to renounce any responsibility for reproducing the discipline, the individual staff member is often free to design their coursework with a high degree of autonomy. As a result, it is quite common for courses to be designed around the staff member's own research or that of their students, leading to a tendency for graduate courses to be tightly focused but highly idiosyncratic, reflective of the particular instructor's personal 'line' on major issues. It is relatively uncommon for these courses to include a comprehensive profile of cultural studies' conceptual history and continuing concerns. In some ways, that is surprising. While a traditional discipline could realistically expect such subject matter to be covered in the student's first degree programme and therefore not be a primary concern of the graduate programme, in cultural studies, as we shall see, that is not such an appropriate expectation and so there is a greater need for it to be covered at the graduate level.

Of course, it is important to acknowledge that there are significant benefits to come from these more focused and research-driven approaches to course design – hence their persistence and their attractiveness to students. But there are also drawbacks. While courses designed in this way are able to generate a considerable depth of engagement with their subject matter, they are unlikely to offer much assistance in the development of a broad understanding of cultural studies as a research field. That might seem a fair trade-off for the student whose own areas of interest happen to coincide with those being addressed in their coursework. For those who are not quite so fortunate, it is not such a fair trade-off. Indeed, when these students are asked to situate their own work, without the assistance of a road map for the discipline, they can experience their predicament as one in which the dimensions of the relevant research field are potentially limitless.

Consequently, it is now common to find graduate students in cultural studies who know relatively little about cultural studies beyond that which will directly equip them to work on the topic they have chosen. This is especially the case for those students who go through a PhD programme in which the dissertation is the only formal requirement. But it is not only a problem for these students. A common complaint among those charged with supervising graduate student projects or teaching graduate level courses is the dramatic variations they encounter in the depth and sophistication of the knowledge of the field that is brought into the classroom with the students. To some extent, I know, this has always been the case – cultural studies has always drawn students from backgrounds in other disciplines or fields. We have become accustomed to dealing with the graduate student from sociology or English or communications studies – and each of these presents particular pedagogic problems. But that is not the problem I am referring to here. Even when I am examining the dissertations of students with first degrees in cultural studies or in closely related fields such as media studies, I find major variations in depth, breadth and sophistication – and my colleagues report similar experiences. The weakness of many undergraduate programmes in cultural studies must be implicated here (and I look further into that in the next two chapters). Many of these programmes are highly fragmented, often (albeit reluctantly) tailored to a market logic which privileges a playlist of disarticulated choices, and lacking a coherent theoretical, historical and conceptual spine that might support an understanding of the epistemological distinctiveness of the field. In the USA, as Michael Bérubé (2009) pointed out, cultural studies courses have found space within other disciplinary locations and may well have to negotiate or even mask their cultural studies orientation. Typically, cultural studies undergraduate programmes produce students who may have an impressive repertoire of intellectual attainments but only a very slim grasp of what binds them all together. Little wonder, then, when these students go on to undertake graduate study, their instructors find it difficult to work out what precisely it is they can rely on their students to know.

This lack of shape and coherence – that is, both at undergraduate level and in the course offerings for graduate students – creates a particular problem in relation to the teaching of research methodologies to PhD students in cultural studies. We are familiar with those criticisms which accuse cultural studies of de-contextualizing theoretical or methodological strategies borrowed from other disciplines, and applying them in ways that do not care to maintain the rigour or precision required of them when used in their discipline of origin. It is probably worth noting that there is a degree of mythology here that serves the interests of cultural studies' detractors and exaggerates the contemporary pertinence of these criticisms. There *are* now cultural studies methodologies which combine empirical and critical approaches in ways that are distinctive (Pickering, 2009). It is also worth reminding ourselves that the task for cultural studies, from the beginning, was precisely to develop methods to do things that had never been done before. That might have involved a bit of what we might now call 'sampling', but it doesn't necessarily, of itself, imply a lack of respect for the integrity of research methods. All of that said, it is true that there is a long history of debates about cultural studies and research methodology. The use of ethnography is the most well-worn example here, and debates about cultural studies' uses of this method go back at least to the 1980s (Nightingale, 1989). While I would still maintain that there are good reasons for cultural studies to have developed its tactic of raiding other disciplines for their methods, it is not surprising that cultural anthropologists should be dismayed if a study of media audiences is referred to as 'ethnography' when it only involves a few hours of home visits and a taped formal interview. As a result of genuine concerns such as these, there is some point to criticism of cultural studies' methodological practices, which accuses the field of being insufficiently rigorous, of selectively appropriating only the shiny surfaces of other disciplines' methodologies, and of applying them without sufficient respect for their methodological integrity. These accusations could also be extended to include the way many cultural studies graduate programmes have approached the teaching of research methods to their students.

There are some significant extenuating external factors here, however[9]. While those teaching graduate students in cultural studies might recognize that students lack a sound overview of the field or a sophisticated understanding of the histories of its foundational concepts and ideas, there are often significant constraints upon these instructors' capacity to satisfactorily address this within the confines of their graduate programme. They are often competing for inclusion in an extremely limited schedule (many programmes I have encountered only offer a total of two or three courses to PhD candidates), they may be faced with a student group that has an impossibly varied menu of highly specific (and sometimes urgent) needs, and they may be working in a school that is dominated by another discipline – communications, say, or English. As a result, when charged with teaching a research methods course to these students, instructors are forced to focus only on the most obvious and pressing methodological gaps. Under the pressure of time and the competing demands from students, these are likely to be taught as a series of freestanding methods, enabling them to be applied, but nonetheless almost unavoidably disconnected from the full theoretical contextualization of their development. The point of such courses is perfectly legitimate, of course – they are often essential in equipping the student to complete their research project. The broader task of providing what might be called a disciplinary background in cultural studies, has been set aside – rarely attempted, let alone accomplished. Indeed, in some systems – and this is related only to those based on a dissertation-only model – even the provision of these gap-filling courses is a luxury. In such situations, typically, it is up to the supervisor to provide a reading list and his or her services as a sounding board and research resource: an informal crash-course in what the student must have read before they can complete their project. The actual experience delivered via such a framework will vary considerably, depending on the expertise and diligence of the supervisor. Further, since methodological training in almost all its iterations tends to be embedded within the management of the major research project, it is almost inevitable that the acquisition of skills and methods becomes an *ad hoc* rather than systematic process; this in turn implies that method is a largely instrumental rather than a theoretical practice.

I want to turn now to the wider question of how all this is going to work out in the long term. I think it is increasingly urgent that cultural studies scholars seriously consider if what we are currently doing is in fact the best way to ensure the continuity of our field of study. Specifically, I think we need to consider the cost of continuing to resist the need to behave more thoroughly like a discipline ourselves – at least in how we design our graduate programmes. To explain why I think that, let me construct a brief narrative of the part that disciplinarity, rather than interdisciplinarity, played in how we got to where we are now.

It would be fair to say that many humanities scholars of my generation were attracted to interdisciplinary developments such as cultural studies because they were frustrated by the constraints on what it was possible to do in the discipline in which they had trained. In my own case, my background in literary studies encouraged me to think that close textual analysis might be a useful methodology to apply beyond the literary text and into popular culture. Within the field of literary studies at the time, however, this was not acceptable. My own PhD thesis ran as close to the line of the admissible as it was possible to get by working on popular American fiction writers J.P. Donleavy, Joseph Heller, Richard Brautigan and Kurt Vonnegut. One British university with research interests in contemporary American fiction refused even to consider supervising such a thesis; it was unacceptable because the fiction was not regarded as sufficiently literary. I eventually found a home for the topic in an interdisciplinary environment and completed my thesis, but my oral defence commenced with the external examiner (who came from literary studies) announcing that, in his view, my thesis should 'never have been allowed to proceed'! In stark contrast to that experience, cultural studies not only encouraged me to test the power of textual analysis on the experiences of popular culture, but provided me with the methods to do it.

My story is in many ways typical of the first generation of cultural studies scholars. In general, coming from related disciplinary backgrounds in the humanities and social sciences, they embraced interdisciplinarity in the first instance as a means of extending the purchase of their home disciplines. In telling such stories, though, it is easy to elide the part played by our earlier disciplinary training in enabling us to benefit from these interdisciplinary initiatives. Most of those who led the interdisciplinary movements that swept the humanities and social sciences from the 1970s on were moving out of disciplines that may not have allowed them to do what they wanted in terms of the focus or subjects of their research, but that nonetheless did equip them with protocols of criticism, research, analysis or argument which endowed their work, even in its new context, with rigour and structure. For example, Stuart Hall has talked about the importance of his critical training in literary studies as a means of helping the first cohorts of students at the Birmingham CCCS to plan and undertake rigorous and systematic research. According to Hall, the centre's development of these students' 'transdisciplinarity' would have been impossible without that training (McCabe, 2007: 23.) This raises a serious question: does the success of the interdisciplinary project actually depend upon the prior possession of a disciplinary foundation? If it does, then that has implications for how we have chosen to go about our business in cultural studies. We may be facing a situation of progressively diminishing returns on our investment in the development of cultural studies as each successive generation we teach come to us, more and more thoroughly as 'interdisciplinary natives'; as such, they stand to acquire less and less in the way of a disciplinary means – by which I mean a rigorously theorized set of research practices – of undertaking their research. Bluntly put, it seems as if we may have erred in expecting a long-term interdisciplinary project to survive without explicitly taking on at least some of the basic characteristics of a discipline – such as a clear set of methodological protocols, a detailed conceptual and theoretical history, and an elaborated epistemology. Or, as Chantal Cornut-Gentille D'Arcy has put it in a sobering analysis of the institutionalization of cultural studies in Spain, the 'blurring of disciplinary boundaries (a major imperative of the original Cultural Studies project) is exacting a high price' (2009: 867). For cultural studies, she suggests, the perpetuation of its heroically undisciplined character may actually be impeding the development of the characteristics which would assist its survival.

It is worth considering, then, if this is the unintended effect of cultural studies' reluctant disciplinarity. That is, while all the institutional pressures and pedagogic demands result in cultural studies behaving like a discipline in certain ways – how we try to structure our undergraduate curricula, for instance, or how we assess postgraduate dissertations – we have acquired an ethical orientation which opposes disciplinary structures with sufficient force to make us uncomfortable about reproducing the disciplinary field: that is, in providing a comprehensive *training* (and this word exposes a crucial fault line, my view) in the analytic protocols, theories, histories and methods of cultural studies. Hence, the refuge in the notion of the 'undiscipline' – in a mythology which enables us to tell our students why cultural studies does not choose to think of itself as behaving like a discipline. While we have conclusively established the usefulness of interdisciplinarity as an interventionary tactic, we may also have made use of it in ways that perhaps misrecognized what it can and can't do. In some ways, what cultural studies has done over the last couple of decades could be seen as constituting an informal and unintended longitudinal experiment – using cultural studies as the means of testing what kinds of results a thoroughly interdisciplinary approach to graduate training can generate. As I have indicated above, some of the results of this longitudinal study that are now becoming visible are cause for concern.

SO, WHAT NEXT …

As a means of enabling our graduate students to emerge with a stronger background in the field, equipping them to contribute to its reproduction and its development, we need to devote greater attention to providing them with an account of the field, a theoretical history if you like, which teaches them the concepts and concerns that have been the distinctive territory of cultural studies. In addition, we need a more substantial commitment to providing training in the research methods than the practice of cultural studies has so far required. Obviously, this is much easier said than done. Mind you, there should be no problem in serving up the theoretical history: I am merely one of the names on the ever-increasing list of those who have written introductions to cultural studies that frame their account of the field in historical terms. In addition, during the 1990s, it became routine for cultural studies books dealing with all kinds of topics to present an opening chapter which rehearsed the history of the field. By the end of the 1990s, that tune was so familiar, one was tempted to sing along. Notwithstanding the wealth of available resources, however, it is relatively unusual to find a course (at either undergraduate or graduate level) that organizes itself around key concepts, or around a narrative of theoretical development. As we shall see in Chapter 3, it is far more common for courses to be organized around the writings of particular theorists, and thematized around the elaboration of theoretical categories such as identity or representation. One has the suspicion that providing a clear account of the conceptual development of the field looks just a bit too easy and routine. It is crucial, nonetheless, because it is precisely this kind of knowledge that our graduate students most often lack.

The issue of how to teach cultural studies' research methods, though, is a much thornier one. Cultural studies may have its own corpus of theory, it may have its own politics, but it doesn't have an exclusive methodology. Earlier on, the textual analysis of popular culture texts may have represented what cultural studies had developed so far as its own distinctive methodology (certainly, it became the core target of choleric accounts of cultural studies from within the empirical social sciences – for example Ferguson and Golding (1997)). With cultural studies' early focus so concentrated upon media texts, it was entirely understandable that textual analysis should have been such a major component of the cultural studies research and analysis published in the 1980s and 1990s. That has changed, however, and there are now many more approaches and methodologies in play. Textual analysis has become a more routine methodology and it is now much less common to find something published in cultural studies that foregrounds textual analysis as its primary attraction[10]. Therefore, we need to do much more than simply introduce the practices of textual analysis to our students. The question is: if we want to properly equip our graduate students for cultural studies research today, what should we be teaching them?[11].

As our critics like to tell us, it is one of the peculiarities of cultural studies as an interdisciplinary field (indeed, ironically, a marker of its success at working across disciplinary boundaries) that it is not especially apparent how one actually 'does' cultural studies. Even if we get past the question of 'Why do it?', the question of 'How do you do it?' remains. Cultural studies must be one of the few fields where that problem is openly admitted and referenced directly by the titles of books such as Du Gay et al.'s *Doing Cultural Studies* (1997) and Matt Hills' *How to do Things with Cultural Theory* (2005). (I don't recall too many academic books dealing with 'How to do' literary studies, or history or cinema studies.) The trouble is, of course, that neither of these books actually lay out a set of methods. *Doing Cultural Studies* provides a model of cultural studies analysis effectively as a finished product; to find out how the authors generated that outcome requires the reader to do a little more work.

It might be useful to talk briefly about that process. I used *Doing Cultural Studies* many years ago in a capstone (final year) undergraduate subject that attempted to do both the things I have been calling for here: it outlined a theoretical history and it taught students a range of research methods. *Doing Cultural Studies* was there for the latter purpose. *Doing Cultural Studies* is organized around Hall's 'circuit of culture' model which argues that the analysis of culture demands engagement with five 'major cultural processes': representation, identity, production, consumption and regulation (1997: 3).

The book recommends attention to as many of these processes as possible in order to generate the kind of conjunctural analysis that cultural studies requires in order to understand culture as a dynamic and articulated process rather than as a series of freestanding objects, practices or sites. The authors then provide a 'cultural studies' account of the Sony Walkman that draws on approaches from cultural history, oral history, political economy, design history, production studies, as well as textual analysis. Each chapter takes as its starting point a particular conjuncture in the circuit of culture, but the methods used to generate the information are still not necessarily obvious. While it doesn't, then, provide a primer on how to do cultural studies, it does provide a demonstration of what the desired outcome should look like for anyone interested in doing cultural studies.

With my students, I discussed how the authors might have generated the information they used as a means of teaching them the point and function of the methods involved. These were students heading for an honours programme, and in many cases had graduate study in their sights, so it was important they had direct experience of applying these research methods as well as the opportunity to explore the process of selecting what would be the appropriate methods. Their final assignment was modelled on the Walkman study; they were to design a research project dealing with a site, or text or practice of their own choosing. This involved developing a research plan, over a period of weeks and both in and out of class, that would generate the information they were seeking. Their choices of topics ranged broadly, for example, from the subcultural practices focused on a city tattoo parlour to the activities of a car club devoted to the VW Kombivan. The assignment required the students to nominate the moments in the circuit of culture through which they were going to approach their research subject, and outline how each of these moments would generate research opportunities and problems for them. They were expected to address all of the moments Hall nominates in the circuit of culture model, even if they proved unproductive in terms of what information they might generate. They brought their research questions to class where I helped them discuss how they might be addressed, methodologically. Sometimes this involved an elaborated outline of the methodology needed, and its theoretical context, as well as a list of suggested background reading. At the end, the students didn't present a paper with the research completed – there was no time for that. Instead, they presented their research plan: a paper which outlined their research questions, the approaches proposed, the methodologies selected and the resources consulted to inform all of this.

This was a start, I thought, and the approach of placing a particular problem at the centre of a discussion of methodological choices was an effective way of getting students to think about method as fundamental to their practice. It is only one example, though, of how deliberately we need to address the contingent manner in which cultural studies research can develop. And that is probably the key point, the importance of balancing an acknowledgement of such contingency against the need to provide students with a repertoire of established approaches from which to make their choices. Balancing these two principles is genuinely difficult in practice because they are essentially contradictory. At various times cultural studies has been enthusiastic about a range of methodologies taken from elsewhere – content analysis, cultural history, policy studies, production studies have all been both fashionable and useful methods for those working in cultural studies at various times. This is not simply a process of *bricolage*, however, it does have its rationale. Faced with a problem such as attempting to deal more effectively with audiences' consumption of popular cultural forms, it is characteristic of cultural studies that it should look around and see what other disciplines have to offer them here. Hence, the early interest in screen theory, then ethnography and, now, in material culture studies of consumption. So, there is a level of curiosity and opportunism which comes from the field's flexibility and which is significantly enabling. While it generates benefits at the level of practice, however, it raises pedagogic difficulties for those wanting to map the field for a contemporary student.

In the end, of course, it is unrealistic to expect anyone teaching cultural studies to have a permanent and unchanging list of the methodologies commonly used by cultural studies research. It might be wiser to teach how one approaches the problem of method by closely examining how the choice of methodology is related to the research question; this should be initiated by the teaching of a range of cultural studies research questions in order to outline the point and theoretical origin of each methodology as well as the process of its application. It would also help if this was done with a stronger historical consciousness. As a result of what I see as their poor command of the history of their own field, our postgraduates are in danger of naïvely reinventing the wheel, of not recognizing established ideas or formulations and then having to do the work from scratch themselves, only to be told, eventually, that it has all been done before.

In addition, it should be said, there are methodologies that are common to the humanities fields and disciplines in general, and it is regrettable that we have been particularly disinclined to provide proper training in these. Cultural studies academics need to properly understand historical research methods, for instance, as so much cultural studies now involves some element of historical research. However, in many cases, the use of history is largely gestural, operating more as a discursive frame or a stylistic choice rather than as a thorough observance of the established research protocols of the discipline of history. This is not only due to the fact that many of these students simply have not been taught the appropriate research methods (although that is bad enough!). It is also a consequence of cultural studies' principled insouciance about the observance of such rules which, in turn, is a product of its disinterest in the 'discipline' part of interdisciplinarity. The fact that we are borrowing methods doesn't entitle us to disrespect the protocols of usage which provide them with their integrity and authority, but the legacy of the undiscipline does dispose us that way. By way of comparison, we are much more committed to demanding sophistication and rigour from our theoretical work. Research design and research methodology – particularly (still!) if it has an empirical component – seem to regarded as belonging to a different order of intellectual enterprise and thus do not garner sufficient respect. My guess is that what I have observed as the lurking disrespect for something called Research Methods may be a direct result of the lurking fetishization of something called Theory. Perhaps it is the case in some quarters of cultural studies, that research is what you have to do if you aren't good enough to do theory.

CONCLUSION

I referred earlier to Chantal Cornut-Gentille D'Arcy's discussion of the institutionalization of cultural studies in Spain. Her account, published in a special issue of *Cultural Studies* devoted to transnationalism and cultural studies, while drawing on quite a different institutional history for the field, resonates against the descriptions of the institutional fate of cultural studies in the USA referred to in Chapter 1 (Bérubé, 2009; Shumway, 2010). Cornut-Gentille D'Arcy points to the 'ambivalent position of Cultural Studies in Spain':

> [o]n the one hand, it has become all the rage as a trendy critical practice in many areas of study (despite the (too often) partial, watered down versions of cultural criticism used). On the other hand, it a historical dead-end, with literally *nothing* to show for itself (no buildings, no schools, specialized courses, curricula modules or ongoing funding), excepting the research and dedication of an irreducible core of convinced adepts, scattered in various Spanish Universities. (2009: 864)

A key factor which has contributed to this situation, she suggests, has been the denial of 'the intellectual and physical space necessary for fostering creativity, intellectual growth, institutional support and opportunities' (866), that is, a 'room of one's own', or the space accorded to a discipline within the university. In ways that reprise the argument I have been making above, she highlights the historical and institutional short-sightedness of cultural studies' refusal of the opportunity of becoming a discipline:

> the success of an interdisciplinary enterprise is measured in terms of its capacity to wedge a place for itself in departments as a new discipline. Thus, at the end of the road – as well as along the way – is *discipline*, with its usual array of requirements, examinations and certifications; with training in specialized skills, vocabularies, canons and the recognition and advancement of specialists in the field. (865)

Cornut-Gentille D'Arcy clearly has no illusion about the limits to what disciplinarity might enable, however: 'training in disciplinary practice leads knowledge transmitters *away* from the study of the relation between culture and society and towards the accumulation of expertise' (866). One result of this, she notes acerbically, is the creation of the 'movie-star' scholar, interested only in self-promotion (for what it's worth, I don't think our lack of disciplinarity has totally protected us from this). Nonetheless, her account of the situation in Spain highlights very much the same contradictions with which this chapter has been concerned and which limit the progress of the interdisciplinary project of cultural studies.

As I said at the beginning of this chapter, what I see as the limitations to the implementation of interdisciplinarity do not only apply to cultural studies. It seems to me that the humanities generally – and especially the humanities, since interdisciplinarity has had a particular impact and provenance in this sector – may be entering a phase when they need to think about the long-term prospects of an interdisciplinary field. Can such a field be sustained indefinitely without mutating into something else? Is Cornut-Gentille D'Arcy correct, that this must be a cyclic process through which interdisciplines consolidate their practices and conceptual fields to become disciplines – even if only for a short time, before they are hit by the next wave of transdisciplinary transgression? Disciplines are very good mechanisms for reproducing themselves (after all, that is what they were designed to do), but there is reason to think that the interdisciplines are not designed to do this very well at all. In most cases, the interdisciplinary enterprise is an interventionary one, tending towards a contingent institutional embodiment rather than a more long-term programme of development and self-fashioning. What has not been much discussed is what might be the next step after this institutional moment has passed, and the interdiscipline is operating more or less just like the disciplines it displaced. There are some very different options, it seems to me. Should the progress of an interdiscipline be monitored so that it does not simply engage in a cyclical process of becoming another established discipline? Or, alternatively, is that a desirable outcome towards which we should be working? While I am interested in these questions as they relate to the future of cultural studies, they have much wider ramifications than this and affect some of the major fields of study within the humanities.

In my introduction to this book I suggested that cultural studies may have acquired some of the negative aspects of a discipline – its sense of boundaries – without enough of the positives – a fully developed epistemology that can be taught as method. Even though cultural studies has had its border skirmishes about who gets to call themselves cultural studies, that may still be a little harsh. As we have seen, there are significant obstacles to the construction of a programme of training in research methods for cultural studies; among these is the fact that cultural studies has indeed continued (and must continue) to remain open to new approaches, new methods and new insights. To completely put that aside in order to establish a set agenda for research practice is obviously inconsistent with how the field has developed over its history. Nonetheless, as we continue to admit graduate students to our care, and as we accept the responsibility of equipping them to take on teaching and research careers of their own, we do need to think about the problems this situation raises. If we don't do a proper job of training those students (and I recognize that agreeing on what this might be is precisely the problem), how will they be equipped to train the generation after them? It is not only our obligations to our students that should give us cause for concern, but also the long-term prospects for the field's development or survival.

Over the years since cultural studies began, many of us have worked hard within our own universities and countries to achieve acknowledgement of cultural studies as a legitimate field of study so that those who work in cultural studies are granted the same kind of institutional status accorded to other disciplinary formations, so that we can continue to be able to teach our students the things that we think matter, so that we can gain access to research funding, and so on. If it was to succeed, much of that work involved us talking to others about cultural studies as if it was a discipline. Once our place in the higher education establishment has been secured, at least for the moment, it becomes a little implausible to continue to indulge in fantasies of our independence from that formulation. And yet, there is still resistance to thinking about what a discipline of cultural studies might do that is different from what it has always done. There is both complacency and denial involved here. While always ready for the work of theoretical elaboration, cultural studies is less ready to reflect on its changing condition as a practice within the university. And yet, as the fields of interdisciplinary thought multiply across the university system (and not just in the humanities), there is a lot to be learnt from what has become of cultural studies as it struggles to negotiate what remains a foundational and difficult contradiction – between its ambitions to remain free of the ties of disciplinarity, and the institutional reality that it needs to embrace at least some of the obligations of a discipline: at the very least, in order to maintain a relationship of good faith with the students it attracts and teaches.

NOTES

1 For an example of the kinds of discussions I have in mind here, see Jennifer Daryl Slack (2005).

2 Other locations where this notion is employed include Clarke's *New Times and Old Enemies* (1991), and McRobbie's *Postmodernism and Popular Culture* (1994).

3 I am indebted to my colleague Anna Pertierra for pointing out the importance of this distinction to me.

4 Eventually, this experiment was abandoned, and these institutions were transformed into universities, similar to the fate of the polytechnics in the UK.

5 Trent was established with a college structure rather than a faculty structure; it was one of the first universities to use the title of cultural studies for one of its departments.

6 See Simon Marginson and Mark Considine (2000) *The Enterprise University: Power, Governance and Reinvention in Australia*. Cambridge: Cambridge University Press.

7 The USA is to some extent another story. As noted in the previous chapter, cultural studies started there much later, it made much more noise when it did, and it achieved much less institutional purchase than it hoped – certainly at the undergraduate level. At the point in time on which I am focusing here, the USA is only a minor player in the development in the field; some of the figures who would lead the field's development in the USA at the end of the 1980s (Janice Radway, for instance), were apparently unaware of cultural studies' existence at this earlier point in time.

8 I am going to operate with a degree of generality here because I don't want to get involved in an invidious process of naming specific examples. Hopefully, what I am describing will resonate sufficiently with the reader's own experiences that specific examples won't be necessary. Then, it is a case of 'if the cap fits …'.

9 An external factor which is of particular relevance to the Australian context, and may be to some extent in the UK, is the virtual disappearance of the research master's degree. While the research MA is not quite such a critical component of the US graduate experience (given the structure and composition of the American PhD), its decline is definitely implicated in what is now emerging as a serious problem with the dissertation-only model preferred in Australia. The research MA used to provide an important

transitional stage for students moving from an honours degree to the much larger task of developing and completing a major research project. The MA also tended to have a course work component, even in programmes where the PhD did not, and so made a considerable contribution to the continuing development of the graduate students' academic background. These days, for a variety of reasons, many fewer students enrol in a research MA and fewer of them are offered; most students go straight from an honours degree to the PhD, reducing the time spent in graduate school by at least a year. This places even more pressure on the undergraduate degree's capacity to prepare its graduates for further study, at a time when these degrees are being increasingly oriented towards responding to student demand rather than the requirements of a disciplinary background. It is likely that the research MA will eventually disappear (although some of my colleagues tell me that there are freestanding MAs that are attracting students, they are few in number). For the humanities in general, one would imagine, the resulting reduction in the time spent learning the field will have a long-term effect if Australia does not adopt something a little closer to the US model of a more comprehensive and directed postgraduate training. At the moment, it seems to me, the decline of the research MA is in part responsible for the problems we are noticing in students' preparation for graduate study over many subject areas – not just in cultural studies. That said, these problems have been greatly exacerbated for cultural studies by the factors I have been reviewing.

10 Outside the field, its influence is substantial. The interpretation of texts has become almost a common mode of public discourse; journalists use it routinely in their weekend colour supplement features, and in Australia and the UK, it gets taught as part of the English curriculum in high school.

11 I realize there is nothing novel about this question. There are, in fact, quite a few books which have set out to address it by outlining core methods and approaches for cultural studies research, some of which directly address the problems faced by research students. A number of them are extremely thoughtfully prepared, and particularly alert to the full range of ambiguities and contradictions which underpin an interdisciplinary research practice. One such example, is Richard Johnson et al.'s *The Practice of Cultural Studies* (2004) and a more recent volume is Michael Pickering's *Research Methods for Cultural Studies* (2009). An

early attempt to address this issue from a range of disciplinary and theoretical perspectives is McGuigan's *Cultural Methodologies* (1997), a well-reasoned articulation of the cultural studies approach to ethnographic method can be found in Ann Gray's *Research Practice for Cultural Studies* (2003), and an introductory level textbook aimed at linking research method with cultural studies theory is Fran Martin's *Interpreting Everyday Culture* (2003). For some of the reasons outlined in this chapter, however, none of these has yet become the standard 'bible' for a genre of cultural studies methods courses.

TEACHING CULTURAL STUDIES

3

As I have already suggested, there are questions about how well our undergraduate programmes in cultural studies are preparing our students for graduate study. I think there are also questions about how well our programmes are serving the needs of undergraduates who are simply taking cultural studies as their major. As suggested in the previous chapter, even where they exist as independent entities, cultural studies programmes tend to be highly fragmented. Also, I think it would be true to say that it is more common now than it was when the field began to find that students are attracted by the topics of our courses, rather than by the fact that the approach being taken is cultural studies. So, we may find our classes full of students who are interested in reality television or celebrity but not particularly bothered about cultural studies. Inevitable, perhaps, as cultural studies loses its 'cool' status to newer arrivals such as new media or creative industries (and we will talk about them more later on in the following chapter), but some of us are finding that we must adjust to the fact that we have fewer students who are excited by their exposure to cultural studies. This is by no means a uniform experience, however; while some report a decline in student engagement, many others report that it is still as strong as ever. Perhaps what this means is that not only is there now much greater variation in students' motivations for doing cultural studies courses, but also that there is much greater variation in the focus and quality of the experience they have when they do. There is evidence to suggest that there is more to these observed shifts than just the cycle of student fashions. I want to raise a number of issues which I think reveal not only a degree of complacency but also an element of elitism, creeping into the teaching of cultural studies.

The teaching of our undergraduates has not been a major field of debate recently in cultural studies in the West, although there is definitely strong interest in Asia[1]. There are Western cultural studies scholars with a major interest in pedagogy, such as Henry Giroux, for instance, but his theoretical work is concentrated on critical pedagogy in the school system. Occasionally, there is a panel on teaching at the large international conferences, but it would be hard to demonstrate that it is a central concern for the field at the moment. As someone who spent the first 20 years of his career designing cultural studies courses so that they might be inserted into, and perhaps eventually define, whole degree programmes, I find this particularly striking. Like many others of my generation, I imagine, the teaching of cultural studies was my point of entry: the design of programmes, the manner of teaching them, and the politics involved in defining a distinctive place for cultural studies within the teaching programmes of each university in which it occurred, was right at the centre of my practice of cultural studies. While teaching remains at the centre of the daily practice of most of those who work in cultural studies, of course, these days it seems to have receded from the centre of our consciousness of what constitutes the field. In this chapter[2], then, I hope to retrieve the centrality of teaching to considerations of the future of cultural studies and raise some questions about how it is currently being done.

THE MARGINALIZATION OF TEACHING

To begin with, I would like to highlight what I would describe as the increasing subordination of the teaching 'mission' (forgive me, but that really does cover it) of our profession in favour of a research career. There are a number of ways of regarding this, of course. In Chapter 5, I approach it as a positive development, as a shift from 'theory' to research. Nonetheless, it does raise some concerns about the future that need to be addressed, and they affect more than just cultural studies. Once, and it is easy to forget this, the teaching dimension of our profession would have been regarded as the more attractive, even the slightly glamorous, component of the job: think of all those campus novels and movies, romanticizing and sexualizing the authority of the teacher, as well as the nature of the teacher–student relation. Today, while this model still informs fictional narratives (recent films such as *Elegy*, for instance), within the profession itself it would be more common to encounter the idea that the most desirable, if perhaps not quite glamorous, activity for a cultural studies scholar is research.

While I would be surprised if this was not found to be the case elsewhere, there may be some degree of specificity in this view, in that it is very much grounded in the Australian context in which I work. Cultural studies has been very successful in establishing itself as a research field in Australia. Despite having come late and reluctantly to the medicalized model of research that has been progressively installed right across the Australian higher education sector over the past two decades, cultural studies has found it a congenial model. Indeed, after some early teething problems – such as a self-defeating penchant, on the one hand, for writing perversely impenetrable prose in grant applications and, on the other hand, for writing the kind of grandstanding assessors' reports that are aimed at obstructing careers rather than developing the field – Australian cultural studies has thrived in the context of the major government funding programmes run by the Australian Research Council (ARC). It has been one of the star performers in the competition for collaborative and industry-focused programmes as well as in those aimed at what the ARC likes to call 'basic' research (that is, purely curiosity-driven research which serves the development of the academic field). Australian universities place a great deal of importance on their research performance, as a result of changes in the way funding is now distributed: where once teaching funds were used to subsidize research, for many years it has been the other way round. Given its success in research, and given the benefits this brings to the university, it is little wonder that cultural studies in Australia has increasingly come to see research as its main game.

In such a situation, unfortunately, it is perhaps inevitable that teaching should be reduced in importance; for some, I suspect it has been reduced to the role of an annoying and demanding obligation that has to be managed or, if possible, avoided entirely by securing a fulltime research-only position. I don't think this is at all unique to cultural studies, but its prominence as a preferred career choice is perhaps more pronounced there because of the number of research centres with an interest in cultural studies and the consequent number of employment opportunities. What is becoming increasingly evident is that this attitude is quite widely held by many newcomers to the profession, such as recent PhD graduates, newly appointed teaching staff, or early career researchers. At the 'State of the Industry' conference hosted by the Cultural Research Network in Sydney at the end of 2009 – a conference aimed at considering the future for cultural researchers in Australia – panels of postgraduate students and early career researchers included speakers who put such a view repeatedly. This, despite the fact that few would seriously contest the proposition that among the most valuable things an early career researcher might do is teach.

It should go without saying that the value of teaching is both personal and developmental. The initial occasion for elaborating the ideas in this chapter was a conference panel I chaired on teaching for the Cultural Studies Association of Australia in 2008. One of the contributors to that panel, Mandy Treagus, reminded us of the personal satisfactions to come from her teaching. When one of her students tells her that she 'sees the world differently' as a result of what they have learnt in her cultural studies class, Mandy said, that achievement makes her job worthwhile. Perhaps because of its classic familiarity, we are in danger of discounting or underestimating the value of this kind of achievement. The other issue, however, is the developmental dimension of the early experience of teaching. There is no better way to understand one's field than to try to teach it to a bright group of undergraduates empowered to question and to challenge the ideas they are being offered. Dealing with that must be one of the most important formative experiences of the university intellectual; not to have experienced it at all seems to me to constitute a significant disadvantage.

There is another consideration here, though, and that is simply how realistic the ideal of a fulltime research career in any of the humanities disciplines actually is in the current environment. In Australia, it is true, and this may be the case elsewhere as well, the number of opportunities for postdoctoral fellowships and for research fellowships in the humanities generally has increased dramatically over the past decade or so. Nonetheless, they are still very few and the chances of picking one up are not good. The centre in which I work (the Centre for Critical and Cultural Studies at the University of Queensland) is staffed almost entirely by fulltime researchers on fixed-term contracts. They are exceptional young academics, having won their funding through the ARC's Australian Postdoctoral Fellowship programme, where the success rate is below 20 per cent, or by picking up one of only two research fellowships regularly awarded by the Arts Faculty at the University of Queensland each year – at a success rate of around 10 per cent. Every year highly promising applicants are passed over for these latter awards. In my centre alone, we would have at least two applicants each year who possess, in my judgement, the intellectual and personal capacities to successfully prosecute a research career in cultural studies. Despite these kinds of odds, I routinely find, when I present talks on research applications and professional development in general, that most of those who attend these seminars take the view that they are entitled to entertain ambitions of a fulltime research career. On the one hand, you might say, 'Good for them! Why not set that goal?'. On the other hand, it is hard not to feel that it is important for them to recognize that a research-only career remains an unrealistic ambition for 90 per cent of the academics working in cultural studies in Australia. In my own case, for example, the past 10 years of research-only employment have only come after decades of full-time teaching.

It is the pragmatics of the situation that worry me most, then. And I wonder how these ambitions are being fed[3]. Just what kinds of expectations are being sold to completing doctoral students and to junior staff members by their supervisors or by their university's research office? Successful ARC applications result in significant funding benefits to the university, and so it is in the interests of Australian universities to encourage their staff to apply; the fact that so few will succeed ultimately does not bother the university much. It should bother us. It raises the possibility that we are going to be filling our teaching programmes with disappointed researchers who regard a conventional teaching appointment as the consolation prize. And it increases the possibility that those who are currently teaching cultural studies in our universities do not believe that the satisfaction teaching generates will play a fundamental role in sustaining them, personally or professionally. We may be looking at a significant change in the structure of our professional orientation which will have the long-term effect of reducing the quality of the teaching we offer our students. Perhaps this is an overstatement – things may be different elsewhere – but that is the conclusion towards which one is drawn from the Australian experience.

CULTURAL STUDIES 101

The second issue I want to raise is definitely relevant to more than just the Australian experience. My views come from a considerable range of encounters with teaching programmes around the world, from reviewing these programmes for their universities, and from service on advisory boards, examiners boards, selection committees and the like. What I have been seeing lately has begun to worry me.

In terms of its scale, the growth of cultural studies does seem to have peaked in most places other than perhaps in Asia. As we have seen, it has a weak institutional presence in the USA notwithstanding the numbers of academics who might personally identify with the field. One would think that the lack of a substantial presence among undergraduate programmes ultimately represents an insurmountable obstacle to further development there (the series of job cuts at US universities that have resulted from the global financial crisis adds another worrying dimension). In both Australia and the UK, at this point, cultural studies is much more secure institutionally, and it has also developed a credible research profile. There are some worrying signs in these locations as well, however. In the UK, the impact of the government's cuts to the funding of higher education is still to be felt but it is highly unlikely to assist cultural studies programmes. In some institutions in Australia – and my own university is one – the numbers enrolled in cultural studies undergraduate and graduate programmes are in significant decline. Students interested in things that once drew them towards cultural studies are now enrolling in media studies, journalism studies, creative industries, sociology – or just leaving the university altogether. There is evidence that this is happening elsewhere as well. There are all kinds of reasons for this, of course (and the following chapter addresses one group of these), and many of them may be institution-specific and thus perhaps not a matter of general concern.

What is of general concern, however, is what I have observed as a shift in the kind of teaching taking place in cultural studies. I think we need to consider the possibility that cultural studies – rather than being the lively critical beast we like to think it is – has wound up generating teaching programmes that look very much like those of the traditional disciplines it was developed to renovate and displace. We could put that possibility this way.

What if, having gained institutional security, career paths, and a level of sectoral credibility, cultural studies has become lazy, unimaginative, and overly deferential to the established canon of cultural studies theorists and authors – at the same time as it has lost interest in the cultures and experiences of its students? How would we know that? Who could tell us? Where might we talk about it? And what could we do about it? I want to present an account of the teaching of cultural studies today that responds to some of these questions.

Let me outline the key components of the kind of shift I have in mind. They include the following:

- a concentration on teaching cultural studies by way of a canonical selection of theorists or cultural studies authors;
- a corresponding shift away from teaching the foundational ideas of cultural studies as conceptual formations developed in response to particular problems; this shift is usually signalled by a dependence on set theoretical readings rather than what I would describe as 'taught' material (that is, where the concepts are explained by way of pedagogic strategies)[4];
- a consequent tendency towards an exegetical mode of teaching, explaining difficult texts to students ill-equipped to read them without assistance;
- a highly contingent (that is, contingent upon the person designing the course) focus on a menu of issues, ideas and political concerns that may or may not be at the core of teaching the discipline (but are at the core of the interests of the individual academic).

There are (at least) two effects that proceed from this trend which go directly to the usefulness and attractiveness of cultural studies to its students. Such teaching practices do not encourage the integration of the students' own cultural capital into the classes, and thus may be responsible for what presents itself as a reduced capacity to generate students' excitement about what cultural studies can do. It is hard for such teaching strategies not to generate an elitist and, I would argue, ultimately mystificatory approach to the teaching of cultural studies theory that privileges the authority of the knowing teacher rather than enables the curious student.

This manner of teaching cultural studies breaks with a foundational tradition that I would suggest was among the factors responsible for its particular character and success; this is especially true of cultural studies in Australia. Whereas cultural studies in the UK and in the USA was established in the first instance as a research or postgraduate field, and although the early days of cultural studies in Australia were also marked by a strong critical and theoretical tradition of independent academic production, cultural studies in Australia largely began as teaching programmes for undergraduate students. As I noted in the previous chapter, it benefited from the establishment of new interdisciplinary programmes in cultural, communications and media studies in the colleges of advanced education (CAEs), the new interdisciplinary universities and the institutes of technology that began appearing from the early 1970s onwards. Cultural studies penetration beyond the interdisciplinary, applied and vocational side of the university sector was slow – the traditional universities gradually came on board from the end of the 1980s (the University of Queensland was the first, in 1989), with the most recent, Sydney University, only signing up in 2006! However, they were important programmes and their success was often a fundamental factor in the survival of the arts and humanities faculties in their universities. Seen as more contemporary and less ivory-towered than traditional arts faculty subjects and usually focused in the first instance on various forms of media, taught in ways that catered to the particular needs and cultural capacities of their student cohort (their class and educational backgrounds were not those of the traditional university student), cultural studies programmes' appeal for university administrators lay primarily in their demonstrable ability to generate strong student demand in an expanding, but competitive, sector.

This is the common element which links the Australian experience with what has happened elsewhere. Most people developing cultural studies teaching programmes have recognized the strategic importance of student demand and used it as a key argument when seeking support for the establishment of cultural studies in their institutions. The source of that demand did have its peculiarities, but underlying all the institution-specific considerations was a number of common factors. Necessarily, as well as in principle, these early cultural studies programmes were taught in ways that explicitly and deliberately built on their own students' popular cultural capital; their focus upon the media and popular culture enabled students to immediately engage in a conversation with the discipline. As a result, students found that cultural studies was empowering and enlightening, and that it explicitly valued their own experiences. Significantly, too, because cultural studies was so often articulated to vocational programmes such as journalism or film and television production (at a time when these sectors of the media were growing both through commercial development and through supportive policy settings), there was the pragmatic argument that this kind of degree programme could lead to employment. While that certainly helped attract students, it also helped to ground cultural studies programmes in some kind of material formation: there was always an industry to address, not only an abstracted notion of culture.

As I noted in the previous chapter, my own undergraduate background was in English literature, where there was, at the time I studied it, virtually no acknowledgement that the student might come with any useful knowledge at all. The discipline of English was taught in ways that were unashamedly elitist (not all students, it was noted, were possessed of the appropriate sensibilities), mystificatory (literature was not theorized, instead its ineffability was offered up as one of its constitutive qualities), and canonical (there was an hierarchized body of materials students would study and respect, but not fundamentally challenge). I found, of course, that cultural studies was not like that. Indeed, as I said before, for me and for many others who came to it from English, cultural studies provided a welcome corrective to the approaches taken through English: it was not elitist, it was not mystificatory, and it taught concepts rather than a canon. As a result, students quickly acquired confidence in their capacity to understand its modes of knowledge and to apply them directly to material forms and practices. If we now return to the present, some of what I see in contemporary cultural studies programmes reminds me more of my undergraduate experience studying English than of my early experience teaching cultural studies.

Let me give you a sense of what I am talking about, but without getting into the complications of naming an actual example. What I have in mind can be typified by a particular version of the generic first year introductory class, let's call it Cultural Studies 101 (CS101), organized around a menu of standard conceptual topics – identity, representation and so on. These concepts will be taught through a combination of lecture and tutorial, and supporting readings will be set for each week. In CS101, these readings are notable for their improbably high level of theoretical sophistication: the reading will be from Judith Butler, say, or Stuart Hall. This, despite the fact that the chosen readings are clearly aimed at problematizing established theoretical positions that the students have yet to understand. Such readings are not at all concerned, nor should they be, with introducing these positions to the neophyte. Their function in CS101, then, cannot be pedagogic; rather, they serve to signify the sophistication of those who designed the course. Faced with such material, the student is ill-equipped to do what their tutors expect of them to do: to analyse, discuss and argue with the set reading. Before any of that can happen, the reading has to be explained to them and so the class turns into an exegetical performance in which the knowledge of the teacher dominates. While that might satisfy the teacher, for the students it only demonstrates their inadequacy in dealing with this subject matter unassisted. Rather than finding CS101 engaging, empowering and enlightening, they could be forgiven for seeing it pretty much the way I saw English 101 at the University of Sydney in 1965 – as an elitist and mystificatory domain.

In my opinion, there are a lot of courses like CS101 in which cultural studies has become a domain where theoretical material is foregrounded for its own sake rather than for what it might enable the students to do or understand, where the students' own cultural capital is given lip-service but implicitly undermined by the use of inaccessible materials as introductory readings and the main focus of discussion, and where students are increasingly registering their alienation from the subject matter as well as the manner in which it is taught.

I noted earlier that a version of these remarks was used to introduce a panel on teaching that I chaired at a conference in 2008. While my description of CS101 was certainly seen as provocative, it was also clear that those listening did recognize it[5]. Postgraduate students, in particular, attested to its widespread influence, and some spoke of their discomfort in teaching it. Working as sessional tutors, often in more than one university at a time and thus dealing with multiple bureaucracies, student demographics and institutional expectations, creates particular difficulties which a number of postgraduates at the conference, and in emails subsequently, outlined. They reminded me that their situation as teachers was among the most exposed and the least empowered: they were overwhelmingly charged with the responsibility of teaching large, often compulsory subjects which they had played no part in designing and about which some expressed serious misgivings. They had to deal with what seemed to them to be legitimate student complaints without having any power to recommend a response, let alone implement improvements. Furthermore, the sophisticated character of the course readings tested their abilities to the limit because of the high degree of exegetical performance they required for the tutorials. Judging from their comments, it seems likely that the problems in course design I have been describing have impacted disproportionately on sessional and inexperienced teachers.

OLD NEWS AND BAD NEWS

I am sure there are a lot reasons for this situation that are external to the field; for a start, it should be acknowledged that there have been enormous changes to the educational marketplace in which cultural studies must now make its pitch. Some of what cultural studies once offered as important new insights, as David Morley was quoted pointing out earlier, have been integrated into the common language of the media and of public debate. It is not surprising, then, that what we have to say doesn't always generate quite the spectacular reaction it used to. Nonetheless, such a situation does point to cultural studies' considerable success in insinuating its way into the discursive repertoire of our public culture. In particular, and again this is something we may have noted but does not get talked about much outside the staff common room, cultural studies has achieved extraordinary success in infiltrating secondary school curricula in the UK and Australia – in English, media studies, and film and television studies. This directly affects student demand as well as their expectations of our courses when they come to the university.

These courses, by and large, are not what they were. One certainly doesn't pick up the excitement that cultural studies generated at the beginning. Admittedly, turning on the bells and whistles in the early cultural studies courses was, in retrospect, a piece of cake. Students were interested in popular cultural forms but, at the time, unused to being allowed to study them; they were delighted to find that their own interests and knowledge actually counted in cultural studies (they never had in school!). Suddenly culture was a process that was open to analysis; it was neither a given nor a mystery. As teachers, charged with demonstrating how culture could be analysed, we were especially fortunate because we had a handy party piece available to us. When we introduced our students to semiotics as a simple technique of textual analysis, we could cruise over a wide range of popular cultural texts, demonstrating the kinds of information this analytical tool could generate. Teaching semiotics at the same time as we investigated what it could tell us about contemporary popular culture had the dual benefit of making us appear both knowledgeable and cool. Better still, it was not long before the students could do it too, and so our knowledge was attainable rather than elite.

As time has gone by, however, our success in disseminating and popularizing cultural studies approaches has led to the loss of this party piece (and some others as well). As I said earlier, high school curricula in Australia and the UK picked up semiotics years ago. John Fiske's series of textbooks, Studies in Communication, which included his own *Introduction to Communications Studies* (1980) as well as Fiske and Hartley's *Reading Television* (1978), was originally designed for an emerging British cross-over market of senior high school and junior university students. That happened towards the end of the 1970s. These days, most Australian high school students will encounter some version of semiotics before they even get to their senior years. Not only has this robbed us of some of our most successful teaching content, but the way most secondary schools teach semiotics has killed it stone dead. Similarly, with some other cultural studies approaches to textual analysis intended to deal with the politics of the text – with issues of representation and power. From the mid-1980s onwards (and again, this generalization needs to exclude the USA), all kinds of cultural, critical and literary theory that had once been the exclusive preserve of the university migrated into senior school curricula where, largely, it got turned into restrictive formal templates in order to enable students of all levels of ability to make a fist of using it. Over time, that has produced a situation where teachers hated teaching it, and students hated learning it.

This is a long story which I go into in more appropriate detail elsewhere (Turner, 2008b) but I argue that eventually what was left of this truncated body of cultural and critical theory got reprocessed into a crude form of critical discourse analysis that turned all texts into encoded forms of politics – privileging meaning at the expense of pleasure while reducing the processes of analysis and interpretation to a ritualistic game of naming 'the discourse'. Everything, from the most idiosyncratic to the most formulaic of texts, got put through what came to be called the approaches of 'critical literacy' to find the discourses within which the text's politics were embedded. Along the way, I would also argue, this approach messed up another useful pedagogic tool for us – the notion of discourse. In most Australian states, the version of 'discourse' taught in secondary school was such a muddled distortion of the idea we teach (in most places, it became synonymous with what we would have once simply called a theme), that it was almost useless to us and had to be re-taught when students came to the university.

Suddenly, then, all the exciting new things we had been able to tell our students were no longer news. Not only that, but some of these approaches had been so mercilessly flogged at school that they had now become, as it were, 'bad' news. Foremost among the bad news (at least in the UK and Australia) was anything to do with the politics of texts. Most of our students had heard nothing but lectures on the politics of texts since they were 15! What might once have been a startling and provocative notion had been transformed into such a weary and formalized routine in senior English that, for the best of our students, it had come to signify the essence of dullness. In such a context, it is not hard to understand why many of those teaching cultural studies in the universities felt the need to raise the bar, in terms of the sophistication of what they presented to their students, as a means of differentiating between the high school and the university experience.

Of course, we had always set out to have this kind of influence and so we can hardly whine about it having occurred and thus forcing us to write some new lectures. What I suspect, though, is that we have not paid much attention to the effects of our intervention as the years have gone by. Or, to put it another way, we have not been as ready to accept an ongoing responsibility for monitoring how cultural studies concepts have been employed and modified in secondary school curricula as we were to engage in the debates which resulted in these concepts being taken up in the first place. As cultural studies has become more established, as its institutional locations have become more secure, and as each successive generation of cultural studies teachers have found fewer obstacles between them and their capacity to teach the material they want to teach, a degree of complacency has developed, which generates an unfounded confidence in the intrinsic attraction of what we have to offer. There is plenty of evidence that many of those who prepare first year programmes for cultural studies undergraduates are poorly informed about the preparation their students received in high school. Consequently, it is not surprising that they might therefore overlook the urgent necessity of continually coming up with new ways to make undergraduate cultural studies exciting – as an idea and as an experience.

This is not leading up to a 'decline of cultural studies' narrative. Indeed, the way I see it, we are facing the consequences of the successful institutionalization of cultural studies, not its failure. This fundamental question about the way we teach our students and what we think is important to teach them derives its pertinence from the fact that we are in a position to control both of these factors. If our teaching is failing, or if it has become something in which we have lost interest, that needs to be addressed directly rather than simply folded into either a narrative of decline or a lament about being undervalued or misunderstood. This situation has come about because there is no real danger of losing our institutional location in the immediate future, not because it is under threat. That is not a permanent condition, however. Ironically, it seems to me that the danger represented by a declining interest in teaching is that it may, in the long term, undermine the viability and security of that institutional location. If the strength of student demand for cultural studies was fundamental to its institutional success, the failure to maintain the quality of the teaching of cultural studies could prove a fatal weakness.

Here I want to return to the issue I raised at the beginning – the ascendancy of research as the preferred professional domain for today's cultural studies academic. As I noted earlier, the restructuring of public university funding mechanisms in (at least) the UK, Australia, Canada, Singapore, Hong Kong and New Zealand has driven academics towards research as a necessary response to the under-funding of teaching. This situation has its structural and institutional determinants, and these funding regimes send clear messages about how we should prioritize among our various activities. It is not surprising that one result seems to be the erosion of the time made available for, and I would suggest even the importance accorded to, the development of teaching programmes. These pressures are serious and systemic contributing factors which reinforce the more discipline-specific tendencies underlying the complex of conditions I am describing here.

All of that said, the widespread prevalence of CS101 can't merely be sheeted home to the workings of external or institutional determinants. More importantly, while I would argue that the danger it represents is serious, we have the power to address it. Of course, I acknowledge that many of those who have developed courses which would fit the description of CS101 have done so in the service of sincerely held and highly committed academic positions. Debates in my own university about how best to frame our cultural studies teaching have exposed genuine and legitimate differences of opinion about precisely the kinds of issues I have been discussing here. We all agree on providing students with a strong theoretical background and a sense of the shape of the field; we don't necessarily agree on how that should be done. Consequently, I accept that an argument has to be made which demonstrates the costs of the strategy I have labelled CS101. A short digression might suggest the kinds of concerns such an argument would raise.

A few years ago, I was fortunate enough to be asked to serve as the external examiner for Meaghan Morris's cultural studies programme at Lingnan University in Hong Kong. Among the many interesting opportunities this role provided was the reading of samples of student work each semester. I learnt an enormous amount from these samples: about how cultural studies theories played out in a non-Western context, for a start, but much more dramatically about the students' own popular culture. Hong Kong popular culture is just plain rich, and the students' identification with and investment in Hong Kong cinema in particular was remarkable. At the end of the three years I served in this capacity, I had received an education myself. What was striking and admirable about the Lingnan programme was how closely it worked with the students' own experiences, their own cultural capital and political concerns. The Lingnan students are very much like the ones I started teaching in the CAE sector back in the 1970s; first generation university students, low levels of class capital, not necessarily academically gifted but passionately engaged by cultural studies' demonstrable capacity to help them understand their own culture. The programme didn't soft-pedal the theoretical demands upon their students, but it deliberately and effectively worked on the connection between cultural studies' knowledges and the students' own engagement with their own popular culture. That this connection was productive was abundantly clear from the things I learned about Hong Kong popular culture from reading their scripts. Unfortunately, I don't think I would learn that much about the students' own culture if I was to take such a role in CS101. This is the element that has been lost and something we should regret.

A second observation I wish to make from this experience relates to the kinds of performance required from the students. The Lingnan assignments asked students, in effect, to use cultural studies methodologies to produce new knowledge; they involved the application of what they had learned to a research question they devised themselves. The results demonstrated that cultural studies had enabled them to learn something new about their own experiences, location or patterns of consumption. The typical CS101 assignment tends not to be like this; instead, it is more likely to require students to demonstrate their capacity to perform a form of critique. That is, they will be asked to critically assess a text, a practice or a theory against the theoretical models to which they had been exposed. I'll admit that this was an approach that just about everybody used, in the beginning, at least some of the time; routinely, we would send students off home to the suburbs to write an ideological analysis of *Ferris Bueller's Day Off* or *Miami Vice* without much concern that many of the outcomes of this exercise were simply skilled performances of ventriloquism. Students gave us what they had learnt we wanted, and we were unconcerned by the fact that this was a deeply inauthentic exercise to require them to perform. Perhaps some students benefited from the experience, but the possibility that many of these students learned something new is probably remote.

Cultural studies has largely moved on from being dominated by this kind of practice. It would be wrong to regard contemporary formations of cultural studies as simply the ground for endlessly performed, endlessly subtle refinements of, theoretical critique – even though this has been the element of our work most often noticed by cultural studies' detractors, particularly those in the social sciences. Of course, there remains a place for critique in the field and I will return to the importance of that in the next chapter, but there must also be more to cultural studies than that. Nonetheless, the critical imperative lives on comparatively unchallenged in CS101. The typical writing assignment is aimed at inculcating a habit of mind in which cultural studies is primarily involved with the development of the capacity to engage in a particular mode of criticism of existing or established positions rather than with their application or, indeed, with the generation of new knowledge. Worse still, this is usually an exercise in which the theoretical outcome of the critique is already known in advance; whatever the question asked, the students are left in no doubt as to what the appropriate answer should be. The process through which they arrive at that answer is the crucial factor – that is, how accurately and precisely the required critical moves are performed.

This highlights what remains a problem in the practice of cultural studies, which is the blurring of the distinction between critique and research. This is not confined to the domain of CS101 but also affects many publications and conference presentations in the field. The residual legacy of literary studies (and perhaps also, if to a lesser extent, that of other 'aesthetic' disciplines such as art history or film studies) is legible in this stubborn preference in some quarters for seeing cultural studies as primarily a mode of incipiently evaluative criticism. This preference is also implicated in one of the more unpleasant symptoms of such an approach – the personalized evaluation of individual cultural studies theorists and practitioners through the critical analysis of their theoretical/political positioning (the demonization of John Fiske still strikes me as a good example of this). As a mode of academic bloodsport, this is not a long way from the aesthetic 'placing' we endured as literary studies students when we were accused of being personally incapable of responding in a sufficiently sensitive manner to the complex texts in front of us. An elitist and mystificatory tactic, the remit of which is entirely contained within the internal politics of the academy, it is one that should have no place in a discipline which takes seriously the value of a collaborative project of better understanding the construction of the experiences of everyday life through open and interdisciplinary enquiry and research.

CONCLUSION

Teaching, perhaps, amplifies problems within the practice of the field because it can't help but consolidate tendencies into templates or prescriptive structures. The teaching of cultural studies has long been among its strengths: the field's theoretical mobility and its genuine interest in the details of contemporary popular culture have enabled it to respond, rapidly and in informed ways, to cultural change and thus speak, remarkably directly, to the concerns of its students. However, if the evidence of our teaching practices is any indication, some of that mobility and much of that interest looks like it has declined significantly in recent years. It is important that such a decline should be examined – both for what it tells us about the teaching practices within cultural studies as well as for what it tells us about the practice of cultural studies more generally.

Let us suppose, then, that there is something to my account – how do we talk about it, and what do we do about it? To turn to the more practical issues first, it is certainly possible, within each institution, to learn from the comments of postgraduates and sessional teachers and to design a more empowered role for those looking after these large and fundamental teaching programmes. They should be better mentored as teachers, for a start. Also, they should be involved in intramural discussions about pedagogy and design so that their experiences feed into the mix; clearly, this is not routinely happening in many universities – particularly, it seems, the large metropolitan universities with large cohorts of sessional teachers. Correcting this, once the problem is recognized, is easily within our grasp.

Dealing with the approaches taken in CS101, though, requires a larger conversation which returns to some basic territory – what is the point of our teaching and what do we want our students to learn from cultural studies? CS101 does not provide acceptable answers to these questions, in my view, and so its widespread occurrence is a cause for concern. My hunch is that the root cause is not disinterest in these core questions (or in poor answers to them), but that they simply do not have a sufficiently high profile within the everyday practice of cultural studies. This is particularly true in environments when the time available for teaching is continually being eroded by other demands – and that has to be the case for most of us. In these contexts, teaching cultural studies has become the 'non-squeaky' wheel in a context where there are plenty of other squeaky wheels competing for our attention.

Working across the sector to generate a conversation within the field about the point and quality of our teaching is difficult. It may, though, be necessary because at least at that level we can get beyond what are often highly personalized internal and local debates about particular courses and their teachers. Unfortunately, for most of us, our networks are either intra-institutional or built around our research interests. There are very few opportunities outside the confines of the individual school or department where teaching strategies, course design and so on might be discussed. This may be due to the competitive structure of the sector – even in systems that are publicly funded, these days we are directly competing against our colleagues for students and the funding that comes with them. Yet, while we also compete against our colleagues for research funds, there is considerable cross-institution collaboration nonetheless, as well as a professional research infrastructure that continually tests our practice against that of the rest of the profession. There is nothing like that through which we might compare and test our teaching practices.

I suspect a factor here is the complacency mentioned earlier; perhaps there is little discussion about teaching because it is more or less assumed that we have sorted it out. We might mentor junior staff or we might not; we might provide a little bit of advice about course design or the techniques required to teach through the web (say), but, really, pedagogy is not on the radar as a cross-institutional, sector-wide issue that must be regularly addressed. Regrettably, too, it is not in the interests of individual institutions to foster a wider, perhaps national, dialogue about such things – although many institutions fund research projects into teaching that are aimed at benefiting their own performance, few would be interested in brokering a discipline-wide dialogue about the teaching of cultural studies in general. In what is now a definitively competitive higher education environment, in whichever nation one works, sector-wide improvements in a particular disciplinary formation cannot be a high priority for any one institution.

The cultural studies journals and conferences are among the few places where such a dialogue might be initiated and prosecuted; hence the panel presented to the Cultural Studies Association of Australia conference, and the earlier version of this chapter published in *Cultural Studies Review* (Turner,

2009a). This earlier version closed with the sentence – 'Let's discuss this'. That wasn't an empty rhetorical gesture; I was really hoping that the article would generate debate; certainly the discussion after the conference panel as well as the responses of some senior colleagues to whom I showed the draft manuscript led me to hope this would be the case. To this date, I am not aware of a single published response to that article. Let's see how we do this time.

NOTES

1 For instance, the Inter-Asia Cultural Studies movement held a workshop in Taiwan in 2008 on teaching cultural studies which was attended by hundreds of young undergraduate teachers; some of the papers were published in a special issue of *Inter-Asia Cultural Studies* (2008; 9: 3).
2 This chapter draws directly on an earlier version of this argument, which was published as 'Cultural Studies 101: canonical, mystificatory and elitist', in *Cultural Studies Review* (2009) 15: 175–87.
3 Here I should acknowledge that while I am not going to deal with it here, this is actually a less important issue, for the sector as whole, than the problem of accepting postgraduates into programmes that seem to offer the prospect of entry to academic employment; in the USA, in particular, that is looking less like a legitimate expectation for those graduating with their PhDs unless they are coming from schools with the best possible reputation.
4 Paradoxically, even while teaching the canon, it still manages to avoid presenting as a discipline!
5 I should add here that the panel included presentations from three presenters – Angi Buettner, Chris Healy and Mandy Treagus – who each in their own way demonstrated modes of teaching that were very different from those I had criticized in CS101, and thus provided clear alternatives in which the students' own knowledges played an important role.

UNINTENDED CONSEQUENCES: CONVERGENCE CULTURE, NEW MEDIA STUDIES AND CREATIVE INDUSTRIES   4

The title of this chapter highlights what I want to suggest is becoming an important issue: that is, the relation between cultural studies and an emerging concentration of cultural and media analysis on what has come to be called 'convergence culture', new media studies and creative industries.

An examination of convergence culture was the subject of a special issue of *Cultural Studies* in which an earlier and shorter version of this chapter was published (2011: 25(4/5)). The examination undertaken in that issue was, to some extent but not wholly, provoked by the influence of Henry Jenkins' *Convergence Culture* (2006), which had argued that the cultures of use and production identified with the convergence of media, telecommunications and information technologies constituted a major social and cultural shift which must be the central object of attention for cultural studies in the future. The argument has had significant currency, partly as a result of its catching the wave carrying the rapid evolution of new media studies. New media studies has, in its turn, argued that the emerging pattern of new media production and consumption amounts to such a significant structural and industrial shift that it demands a whole new version of media studies to accommodate it: hence, Gauntlett's (2007) proposition of Media Studies 2.0 and Hartley's arguments for 'digital literacy' (2009b) noted in previous chapters. New media studies has also focused its analysis of the potential of new media on the opportunities for democratizing media use and access – itself related to media studies' long-running concern about the asymmetrical power relations which have structured the traditional media's dealings with their audiences. Convergence culture and new media studies are both based on a conviction that the new media operate in ways that are more participatory, more community-oriented, and less commercially venal than the 'Big Media' conglomerates that prevailed during the pre-Internet, broadcasting era. Developing slightly later, and then in fewer locations, but nonetheless working in concert with the other two approaches, the 'creative industries' paradigm also draws upon the optimistic, democratizing, arguments used to describe convergence culture and identifies that culture with the technological capacities released by digital media. Creative industries argues that the expansion of the cultural industries through new, grassroots modes of media production and consumption has now placed the economic development of the small enterprises typically connected with these industries in the centre of the next wave of cultural studies[1]. This complex of approaches, *Cultural Studies'* special issue suggests, has gained considerable traction even though it could be said that the claims they generate have outstripped the supply of supporting evidence. Accordingly, while not denying the potential and significance of developments in new media, there remained a need for some critical scrutiny of the claims upon which convergence culture and its companions have been built. Hence, the special issue devoted to 'rethinking convergence culture'.

The provocation for my taking on a related task in this chapter is that among these claims are those which give convergence culture, new media studies and creative industries a direct genealogical relation to cultural studies. I think there is reason to question, if not their connections to the past, certainly their connection to the future of cultural studies. Hence, the question: are convergence culture, new media studies and creative industries, as their advocates usually claim, the next step forward for cultural studies? Or, rather, are they a significant step away from its core concerns? The view I am putting in this chapter is that, by and large, these are fields that are now dominated by concerns and objectives which have little to do with cultural studies. Specifically, they have little in the way of an independent academic or intellectual agenda, but rather see themselves as serving the demands of an industry that seems magically to have shed its association with capital and become unproblematically identified with the people. To present this as an outcome of cultural studies is to seriously misrepresent the point and the purpose of our field.

THE RETURN OF CULTURAL POPULISM

Let's start, then, with the connections to cultural studies' past. Towards the end of the 1980s and into the early 1990s, there was a series of interventions into theoretical debates about cultural studies which highlighted what Jim McGuigan (1992) called 'cultural populism'. As a response to what had come to be seen as an overly deterministic, largely Althusserian, diagnosis of the relationship between texts and readers, some in cultural studies had begun to present arguments which strongly emphasized the agency of audiences in the process of making meaning. In John Fiske's *Understanding Popular Culture* (1989), in particular, this agency spread beyond the textual encounter into the practices of everyday life; the work of de Certeau was used as a means of arguing for the possibility of resistance within such a context. This resulted in a welter of optimistic accounts of the resistant reader or 'textual poachers' (Jenkins, 1992), and so on, challenging the power of dominant culture and retrieving the possibility that the tactics of the individual could satisfactorily resist that power. To some, this was a welcome theoretical development which helped explain why even dominant cultural formations could still produce change; to others, it carried the quietistic implication that capitalism

was OK, as long as we could all come up with our own readings
of popular culture texts. Still others (and McGuigan was one)
protested that the field had fallen under the influence of a motivated but disavowed trendiness which arbitrarily located the
possibilities of resistance in those domains of popular culture
where, it was suggested, that generation of cultural studies
researchers felt most at home.

McGuigan's *Cultural Populism* (1992) was published towards
the end of this moment, and in some ways sealed it off, so it was
an influential and widely read book. McGuigan made a number
of important claims: that the cultural studies movement was
operating with a default setting that privileged 'the popular' in
a relatively unexamined and ultimately sentimental way; that
this facilitated the withdrawal from a more rigorously theorized
and politically 'critical' cultural studies project; and that this
also meant that while many relatively ephemeral but fashionable locations were examined at length, many more important,
disturbing but unfashionable, expressions of the popular were
ignored because they did not fit into the preferred model of 'the
progressive'. So, we had numerous celebrations of the postmodern textuality of *Miami Vice* but no critiques of the regressive
politics of representation in the top-selling British tabloid newspaper, *The Sun*. While there was much debate about *Cultural
Populism*, it arrived at a point when an increasing number of
people within cultural studies were also pushing back against
the 'resistant reader' and 'active audience' model in order to
return to a more nuanced, more critical, and more contingent
or conjunctural account of consumption and the popular
(Morris, 1990). As Ien Ang wrote, it was inaccurate to 'cheer-
fully equate [the] active with [the] powerful' (1990: 247). Many
agreed – and this is something which is often overlooked by
cultural studies' critics (such as Ferguson and Golding (1997))
– that there was a danger in the adoption of research practices
which did not provide clear critical distance between the scholar
and their object. This was further developed by theorizing the
complicated hybrid identity of the 'fan–critic' (Grossberg,

1997) but in most places where this occurred there was little interest in underplaying the importance of the critical half of that identity.

The accusation of cultural populism, though, legitimately highlighted the arbitrariness of some of the choices made for the focus of cultural studies analysis, the apparently motivated investment in the so-called progressiveness of some of the objects of this analysis, and the fact that many of the more regressive but nonetheless dominant and influential aspects of popular culture tended to be ignored simply because they were outside the taste regimes of cultural studies researchers. The 'cool' end of cultural studies, its identification with the more transgressive and lively forms of popular culture, was both its strength and its weakness. On the one hand, it did rescue the popular in ways that understood and accepted popular culture on its own terms; however, on the other hand, it selected the terrain upon which this rescue took place in ways that provoked questions about the legitimacy of the criteria generating such a choice. At the most crude, there was the claim that cultural studies just looked at the things its researchers personally liked, and then helped them to justify their personal preferences by arguing the case for the political progressiveness of those texts or practices. However, as the active audience model gradually resumed its proper role as merely one of the coordinates against which we needed to situate our objects of study, cultural populism lost much (but not all) of its currency.

I suggested briefly in the introduction to this book that we are now witnessing the return of cultural populism in certain aspects of the engagement with convergence culture, new media studies and creative industries. I have argued elsewhere (Turner, 2010) that teaching and research in these areas is marked by features that are similar to those nominated in McGuigan's (1992) critique: by personal investment in the sites of study, by a disinclination to seriously consider the more critical perspectives on the practices involved, and by an improbably optimistic reading of the politics which frame their relation with their audiences. Ironically, while the association with cultural populism might seem like a damaging accusation, I suspect that it would not necessarily be contested by the proponents of convergence culture, new media studies and creative industries. Indeed, that genealogical connection plays an important role in constructing their intellectual legitimacy – particularly when there is not much in the way of other kinds of evidence to support their claims for the potential of the new technologies. Without the cultural studies' genealogical history to authorize the claims made for the democratizing power of a vernacular medium, these claims would look pretty thin.

Academics in cultural and media studies were, of course, among the first to recognize the cultural potential of new media. Furthermore, they have certainly been at the forefront in noticing the growth of what I am describing as convergence culture – where the blurring of the lines between telecommunications, television and information technologies has assisted the emergence, within some sections of some markets, of new forms of community and participation that are made possible by the capacities of new media (social networking, blogging and so on). The scale and significance of these developments have been subject to many rhetorical claims, but much less in the way of investigation or research. Rather, as I have argued elsewhere (Turner, 2009b), there is an established 'digital orthodoxy' which sees the cultures of online participation, media customization and the individualization of consumption as feeding major, progressive, social and cultural change. Attempts to provide a more nuanced or historicized account – to argue that these developments may turn out to be of limited provenance because of socio-economic or other contextual factors, or that they have not in fact resulted in any significant structural shift in the locations of media power so far, or that we might pay more attention to the histories of new technologies in properly assessing the potential contained within contemporary developments – have often been impatiently dismissed as the recidivistic remnants of a 'neo-marxist' cultural and media studies past (Cunningham et al., 2008; Hartley, 2004). And yet there remain good reasons to challenge the claims made about the scale and significance of convergence culture.

Often, the individual commentator's enthusiasm for new media inflates the degree of importance that tends to be attributed to them. To some extent, this may be understandable. Highly volatile, the technological capacities changing rapidly, these industries do resist long-term analysis and so there are many gaps in the evidence which might help us to better understand their use. Faced with that situation, however, convergence culture, new media studies and creative industries have not designed new ways of generating reliable information. Rather, typically, they move into predictive, futurist, mode. Much of the theorizing and much of what is cited as evidence in these debates actually derives from projections of what, in their opinion, *might* occur. As one media historian has commented, 'new media studies may be the first discipline where "theory" does not derive from a study of "the object"; rather the object of new media derives (so far) more from theoretical conjecture than demonstrable impact' (Sconce, 2003: 187). Hence, I suspect, the unusual, indeed surprising, amount of credence accorded to journalistic and popularizing accounts such as those written by commentators such as Clay Shirky (2008) or Richard Florida (2002) in framing agendas and providing arguments for academic discussions. As a result, what counts as evidence in this field is becoming notorious (Brabazon, 2008: 18; Miller, 2009a: 75; Turner, 2010: 126–34) for its departure from the conventional standards of academic research.

It has to be said that reservations about the hype around convergence culture are not new. Back in 2003, Jeffery Sconce, bouncing off an account of a pre-modern example of popular hype, 'tulipmania'[2], had this to say about the early warning signs from what was then called 'digital culture':

> I think most of us would be hard-pressed to think of a discipline in which more pages have been printed about things that

haven't happened yet (and may never) and phenomena that in the long run are simply not very important (Jennicam, anyone?). Of course, only an idiot would claim that digital media are not worthy of analysis, an assertion that would sadly replicate the hostility towards film and television studies encountered in the last century. No-one doubts the importance of digital media as a new form of distribution for the culture industries or as a new mode of telecommunication for bored office workers. The place of digital media in both the political and cultural economies of the future is certain. But, generally, this isn't really what new media scholars are interested in studying. Academic 'tulipmania' can be found in the seemingly endless claims that the internet, MUDS, avatars, virtual reality, TiVO, Palm-pilots and whatnot have led to radical definitions of identity, race, gender, narrative, subjectivity, community, democracy, the body and so on. (2003: 180)

Nothing much seems to have changed in the object of criticism in the intervening years. It is still the case that convergence culture is home to many examples of 'revolutionary discourse' (181) which proclaim that the take-up of digital technology constitutes a major social change 'as if the major structural problems confronting our democracy were merely technical shortcomings' (182).

As an example of the kind of thing I mean, some working in the creative industries model argue that the creative potential embedded in such developments as social networking technologies has the power to set in train an evolutionary process that will eventually displace outmoded political and cultural structures. One of the more extraordinary applications of this idea is to mainland China (for instance in Potts (2010) or Hartley and Montgomery (2009)). As Justin O'Connor, among others, has said, when projected upon the political landscape of China, this programme of 'social and political transformation through creative consumption amounts to the most naive wishful thinking' (in press). From the very early days of the creative industries project, warnings have been issued about the limitations to the claims made about its likely take-up in China. Jing Wang pointed out that the creative industries model depended on a commercialized cultural sphere, whereas in China 'administrative orders rather than the market principle' had been driving media development and convergence activities. Her assessment of the possibility of finding (let alone expanding!) 'regulation-free creative space in Chinese media', is that the chances are 'slim'– 'regardless of the western media hype about "the revolutionary restructuring" of the cultural sector in progress' (2004: 17–18). Some years later, Michael Keane regrets that 'whatever possible benefits result from debates about creative industries in China', they are outweighed by 'a range of negative externalities':

> As Yudice ... has noted, the creative economy serves the interests of managerial classes, entertainment conglomerates, real estate developers, and the holders of intellectual property more than the subordinate classes of civil society. One might expect that the current fashion within the creative industries, particularly within policy and business circles, to diminish if (and when) returns on investments fail to match expectations. (2009: 441)

As I understand them, subsequent developments provide little reason to question this view. Indeed, the Chinese government has taken up the creative industries brand in ways that capitalize on its usefulness to perform the kind of politically and administratively consolidating role we have seen elsewhere in Asia: that is, to relax controls on the market for entertainment and middle-class consumption as a means of deflecting attention from its refusal to relax the control of more directly political activities (the news media, the internet and so on). The dispute with Google in early 2010 could be understood as a clear demonstration of this. Far from setting in play an emancipatory evolutionary process, then, it would be more plausible to argue that the take-up of the creative industries brand seems actually to have helped authoritarian societies such as China and Singapore to stabilize, contain and circumscribe certain domains of consumption as a means of limiting their political effects[3].

Just to make this clear, it is the excessiveness of such claims, their sheer implausibility, that is the problem. I don't think anyone denies that the convergence of media and communications technologies is actually happening. Convergence *culture*, on the other hand, looks to me to be about 20 per cent fact and 80 per cent speculative fiction. The claims made for its significance are as dramatic as they are unconvincing. The danger of generalizing from the behaviour of specific markets, typically the USA, is one of the most obvious problems. This is not yet (and may never be) a global phenomenon, for a start. Around 50 per cent of the world's population would dearly love to experience converging media platforms but would probably be happy to settle for access to a telephone first. Even in the heartland of the rhetoric of convergence culture, the USA, something between 14 and 20 million citizens have no access to broadband and don't look like getting it anytime soon, according to the Federal Communications Commission most recent report on broadband deployment (2010). While virtually all the claims for the democratizing effects of the blogosphere are anecdotal (and drawn with wearying predictability from the same short menu of examples), we actually do have empirical evidence that seriously questions such claims (such as Hindman, 2009).

Elsewhere (Turner, 2010) I have discussed what I regard as the deficiencies in the claims made about user-generated content, and I am not going back over that material again here. Rather, in the remainder of this chapter, I want to explore a much less widely canvassed issue: I want to discuss how the discourse of convergence culture has informed the development of curricula in higher education in recent years, and in particular how has this affected cultural studies programmes.

CONVERGENCE CULTURE, CULTURAL STUDIES AND THE CURRICULUM

The provocation for focusing on this issue is the gradual but, I would suggest, significant rise in the number of undergraduate and postgraduate programmes and of university research centres dealing with the technologies central to convergence culture. This has been going on for some time. However, while many of these programmes first emerged as specializations within media and cultural studies courses, they are now appearing as stand-alone programmes in their own right. Their nomenclature varies but most of these degrees in multimedia, digital media, new media and creative industries derive from, if not directly at least in close relation to, the discourses of convergence culture. By and large, and even though so much of their content has to do with understanding the capacities of digital media and communications technologies, these programmes are not hosted by computing or information technology departments (although some certainly are), but by arts and social science faculties: in schools of media studies, communications and cultural studies, or as majors in the creative arts or media production. Their expansion[4] has been driven by their success in the market for undergraduate students. That market appeal is built upon the perception that the converging new media are 'cool', that they will provide job opportunities in the future, and that these programmes provide training for those opportunities. Consequently, in just about every case I have come across, the undergraduate curriculum is dominated by hands-on training in the use of the relevant technologies.

However, if the training is overwhelmingly technical, the positioning of new media is not. While they are certainly hailed as products of a major technological shift, the new media industries are attributed with a social and cultural significance that most new industries would not ordinarily enjoy. This is where convergence culture comes in, helping to attract a student clientele which is actually not especially technocratic. Indeed, just like many of the students who have flocked into cultural studies programmes since they began, these students are oriented more towards the media, popular culture and the 'alternative' end of the creative arts. Where cultural studies was so successful in attracting these students was through its interest in their own experience of popular culture – in the markers of 'youth culture' that included, for instance, non-mainstream genres of popular music, zines and cult television. Although an identification between youth culture and convergence culture does not necessarily accurately reflect the evidence about the changing patterns of use[5], such an identification has certainly been made, through a focus on the practices of social networking or user-generated content, viral video and so on. The attraction of these practices for the prospective student is reflected in the designing of the programmes and their subsequent marketing.

Among the tenets of convergence culture that are implicated in the successful market positioning of these programmes are the following:

- the fracturing of the production/consumption binary and thus the distinction between producer and consumer, with the consequent framing of small media enterprises as grassroots, creative responses to mainstream media oligopolies;
- the attribution of a politics of democratic empowerment which spreads a romantic, 'alternative', sheen over these small-scale media enterprises, cleansing them of their association with the interests of capital;
- the overarching idea that the new media industries constitute a new domain of popular and participatory creativity (what McGuigan (2006), calls 'cool capitalism') that has been carved out of a space hitherto conceived as hopelessly corporatized, unresponsive to the consumer, and venally commercial.

In this domain, 'creativity' is newly valorized as both the generator and the product of the interactive capacities released for the participatory 'produser' or 'prosumer' (Bruns, 2008). Within this set of approaches, then, new media are necessarily intrinsically creative, vernacular, democratic and consumerist, not only technically but also ideologically: thus their politics are the antithesis of what the 'old' media represents.

The most remarkable thing about the development I am describing, given its origins in cultural and media studies, is how wholeheartedly these applications of convergence culture have articulated humanities' knowledges to what are in significant part business degrees[6], aimed at assisting the development of the so-called 'new economy'. Units dealing with management, marketing and media business are far more common presences in these programmes than units dealing with any aspect of cultural studies. The commitment to 'engage' with media industries (Jenkins, 2004: 42) – in principle a perfectly appropriate ancillary activity for cultural and media studies which has also fed into the establishment of cultural policy studies and the cultural industries model (Hesmondhalgh, 2007) – expands to the point where, for instance, some formations of the creative industries model in particular have come to *define* themselves through (admittedly, among other things) a commitment to supporting the economic development of these enterprises:

> However, this is not simply in terms of the direct employment and wealth creation of this sector – a claim shared by the cultural industries policy discourse and one which still animates most national and local government creative industry strategies. Just as the cultural industries had other public good outcomes – various contributions to cultural and social life – the creative industries contribute to the 'innovation system' of the economy. Unlike the cultural public goods argument, which makes claims on public money based on market failure, the claims of the innovation system – like other infrastructural investments such as transport, R&D and education – are based on enhanced future economic growth. (O'Connor, in press)

Insofar as this is taken up within convergence culture, such a commitment is substantially legitimated by what O'Connor describes as the 'association of "alternative lifestyles" with entrepreneurial innovation' which he locates in the 'new economy' discourse around new media typified by *Wired* magazine, itself a significant anchor point for the rhetorics of convergence culture (in press). Hesmondhalgh refers to this too; he calls it 'business with feeling' (2007: 142). Toby Miller, one of the hardcore sceptics about the creative industries paradigm (he calls them 'creationists'), acknowledges the usefulness of understanding the cultural components of consumption 'and hence of many economic sectors'. But, he asks, incredulously, do we need 'to believe the rhetoric?' Miller points out that the USA was 'the last country' to do just that 'when it bought into Reagan's 'creative society' four decades ago', and then asks:

> What has been the outcome of a fully-evolved fantasy about small business and everyday creativity as the motors of economic growth? Come on down and take your pick of crumbling bridges, dangerous freeways, deinstitutionalized street people, inadequate schooling, and 50 million folks without healthcare. And politics run by pharmaceutical firms, health insurers, tort lawyers, finance capitalists, arms manufacturers, and gun owners – all of whom make many creative outputs, I have no doubt. As for the cultural industries, they remain under the control of media conglomerates and communications firms. (2009b: 96)

There is clearly anger in that kind of response and it is not hard to trace its origins. Convergence culture effectively sets aside cultural studies' longstanding commitment to the applied critique of the social and political effects of an economistic approach to culture, or indeed its longstanding scepticism about any necessary connection between the operation of the market and the public good, as if this foundational stance was just a passing concern – a phase that cultural studies should now just get over[7]. As Hesmondhalgh puts it, instead of this being an instance of the reconciliation of economics and culture, it is rather 'an annexation of the latter by the former' (2007: 144). Especially when located in the context of the performance of Western financial markets over the last few years, at a time when arguably the need for a structural, political and ethical critique of business has never been greater, this, certainly in its most uncompromising representations (such as Hartley, 2008), constitutes a staggering inversion of the politics of cultural studies.

Notwithstanding such criticism, these programmes, and convergence culture in general, still describe themselves as emerging from cultural studies; indeed, it is characteristic for them to claim 'centre stage as cultural studies enters the 21st century' (Jenkins, 2004: 42). The existing models of cultural studies, though, are no longer what are required. It is routine, within the manifestos written for digital media, new media studies and creative industries, to argue that an outdated theoretical model developed to deal with 'traditional' media must now give way to an entirely new explanatory approach[8]: that is, in the end, the justification for convergence culture, new media studies and creative industries.

Some have put this principle into practice. In a number of universities in (at least) the UK and Australia, the morphing of cultural and media studies (occasionally, cultural policy studies) into new media studies or creative industries has taken an institutional form with the rebranding or restructuring of whole disciplines, schools and even faculties. Although, in practice, these rebranded programmes end up either displacing cultural studies programmes in their own institutions, or competing with cultural studies programmes elsewhere, their choice to locate themselves within a history of cultural studies helps to disavow that competition while positioning their particular take on media and culture at what they then argue is the cutting edge of the field. Of course, it is not only those in the creative industries or digital media who have argued for a rethinking of traditional media theory in the light of changes in the media industries and their audiences over the past decade; there are many others who have been doing this as well (for instance, Couldry, 2000; Katz and Scannell, 2009; Lotz, 2007; McGuigan, 2006; Turner, 2010). However, it is only those in convergence culture, new media studies and creative industries who have argued that they now constitute *the* new theoretical paradigm for our fields of study.

What do we find if we test such a claim against the actual content of the undergraduate programmes now in place? I have spent some time examining examples of these from the UK and Australia[9]. They vary considerably in content and approach; the creative industries programmes, for instance, include some that are still focused primarily on the cultural industries, and appear to be making use of the creative industries label as a means of marketing themselves rather than taking on the strategic focus outlined above. Digital media programmes include some which are largely concerned with the visual arts and the technical capacities that digital media provide to the producers of multimedia arts; others focus on the core territory of convergence culture – new platforms for television, user-generated content, blogging and so on. Overall, however, it would be true of virtually the full range of these programmes that intellectually, academically, conceptually, they are far from the cutting edge of our fields of study. What is most immediately noticeable is, on the one hand, their overwhelmingly technical orientation – training is explicitly their focus – and, on the other hand, the thinness of the academic context provided. Clearly, when technical training is required, its provision eats up a lot of the content of the course. Typically, the convergence culture paradigm sets up a small number of core subjects (from one to four, usually, and so, effectively no more than a semester in total), which carry the burden of providing the academic content; these may provide an introduction to a body of relevant academic work (this is usually what happens in the digital media courses) or they may lay out a manifesto for the approach being taken (this is usually what happens in the creative industries). In some cases, there are academic electives or a minor thread of subjects with an academic focus. Usually, however, even though the core courses are likely to have some theoretical content drawn from media history, cultural policy studies, political economy and so on (rarely cultural studies, interestingly), this is usually no more than a brief attempt to enable the students' engagement with an intellectual field as a means of developing a distinct form of knowledge or academic expertise. Instead, the aim is thoroughly instrumental: to demonstrate to students that this degree, unlike other degrees in the liberal arts and humanities, has a training and vocational focus that will properly equip them for employment in what the publicity for one university in Australia calls 'the real world' (which must be one of the rare instances where a university chooses to align itself with those who think that universities are basically useless). The professional majors are the real point of these degrees – in journalism, public relations, advertising, multimedia, digital media production, film and television and so on.

I should make it perfectly clear that I have no fundamental objection to the existence of such programmes; I want to emphasize that I am *not* saying that the university does not have a legitimate interest in training its students for employment. What I *am* saying, first, and as a relatively modest general point, is that restricting the university to serving *only* that function dramatically underestimates what the institution can – should – achieve. Second, and more specifically, and notwithstanding the narratives used to justify the claims for their academic significance, these courses couldn't be further from providing us with a new theoretical paradigm for the development of cultural studies. Indeed, there is minimal engagement with any theoretical tradition at all, there is only a secondary interest in addressing academic educational objectives, and the focus is upon the production of technical skills and capabilities rather than the generation of knowledge or the practices of analysis. If these programmes are to replace cultural studies, and this is what I am suggesting may be their long-term effect, then a great deal stands to be lost. Worse still, if they were to replace the generalist liberal arts and humanities degrees, not only would they be wiping out what has proven the most hospitable location for cultural studies, but we would have also pulled the plug on a fundamentally important intellectual and academic tradition: the one that takes seriously the task of understanding what it is to be human.

TWO STORIES

Should cultural studies worry about this? I think it should, and to indicate why, let me outline two narratives from the development of cultural studies in Australia, both of which lead to the establishment of a particular version of creative industries as the most full-blooded and institutionally successful iteration of convergence culture in Australia. The first narrative begins with the development of cultural policy studies in Australia. Emerging directly from a longstanding policy orientation in Australian cultural studies, cultural policy studies was particularly successful from the late 1980s through the early 1990s. It established itself as a powerful academic paradigm[10] through the work of Tony Bennett, Stuart Cunningham and Tom O'Regan in particular; it also enjoyed considerable access to government departments and agencies. The Australian government at the time was a reformist left-of-centre administration, traditionally the colour of government most interested in securing policy advice. The establishment of the Key Centre for Cultural Policy Studies (a consortium of Griffith University, the University of Queensland and the Queensland University of Technology), was one of very few humanities and social science research centres to be funded through the Australian Research Council's peak programme and so this constituted a significant institutional achievement for cultural studies as a whole. While there was a strong Foucauldian focus to the work of its Director, Tony Bennett, the Key Centre nonetheless took on a theoretical character that was broadly consistent with the key elements in the practice of cultural studies in Australia at the time. As a development within cultural studies, however, cultural policy studies was far from uncontested[11], and partly for reasons that will be familiar: it, too, like convergence culture, presented manifestos about its importance, which claimed that it should be the centre of cultural studies practice in the future. By some, this was seen as simply hubristic; and for others, the proponents of cultural policy studies overvalued the importance of 'talking to the ISAs' (Bennett, 1989) on the one hand and compromised the intellectual and political independence of cultural studies research on the other.

With the replacement of the reformist Labour administration in 1996 by a conservative government relatively uninterested in the cultural industries, the market for cultural policy advice declined. During the Howard government's period in office (it lost power in 2007), the term of the Key Centre's funding expired and the host universities declined to provide any further support. By then, Tony Bennett had returned to the UK to take up Stuart Hall's chair in sociology at the Open University. Cultural studies' credentials as a source of policy research and advice remained relatively intact, nonetheless, even though the federal and state governments now had little interest in seeking outside advice. Industry, particularly the cultural industries, remained interested in principle, but in practice they were reluctant to invest in collaborative research, and so the possibilities there were limited. Cultural policy studies as a named research field (it had never been a major undergraduate area) lost its novelty and some of its momentum over the next decade. In general, it would have to be said that while cultural policy studies continues to be a significant field it would not now be located in the vanguard of new international developments in cultural studies. Its important role as an incubator of Australian cultural studies research projects – a direct consequence of its Key Centre funding – became less significant over the early 2000s, as more cultural studies researchers learnt how to secure their own funding through the Australian Research Council (ARC). Success in this context provided researchers with greater freedom to determine the focus and character of their research projects; once they were less dependent on developing policy-oriented projects to secure funding, the range and variety of projects and approaches expanded. At the same time, and perhaps as a consequence of this, Australian cultural studies continued to build the credibility of its research within the higher education sector, as well as its international profile.

It is in this context that the Australian version of the creative industries brand emerges – initially through the reframing of some teaching programmes in the liberal arts and humanities. Borrowed from the UK Blair government's 1998[12] strategy for rebranding its cultural industries development policy in ways that emphasized their commercial and service dimensions, the rebranding of the Queensland University of Technology's (QUT) arts faculty as the Faculty of Creative Industries was a pioneering move. It should be noted that this arts faculty was in very poor shape, depleted by years of neglect, and littered with dismembered bodies left over from successive mergers and restructures. It was probably understandable if it seemed that little would be lost by giving the dead a decent burial and embedding the survivors in the popular communications and performing arts programmes under the rubric of the creative industries. Initially keen to maintain its identification with the humanities' disciplines, over time the QUT Creative Industries Faculty brand has become more fundamentally identified with its instrumental role: that of training students for employment in the industries concerned. When QUT's Stuart Cunningham led a consortium of universities in a successful application that resulted in the formation of the ARC Centre of Excellence in Creative Industries and Innovation – the CCI – an alignment with industry was central to the application's rationale. Over time, that alignment has increased to the point where now the core concern of the CCI is the provision of information and research services for the development of small to medium sized enterprises in the creative industries. What remains of any broader agenda is tied to a convergence culture rhetoric that attributes to creativity, the network culture and digital media the kind of social, cultural and political importance I described earlier as implausible[13].

The point of this narrative is to highlight a significant change in what cultural studies has been called on to do, over time, through these two instances. As I say, the cultural policy studies agenda was largely in accord with the core activity of cultural studies, what McGuigan has called 'critique in the public interest' (2006: 138), in that it had its eyes firmly fixed on the public good – this, understood as distinct from the political objectives of governments or the commercial objectives of the cultural industries. There was no doubt about what the point of cultural policy studies was. The transition from cultural policy studies to the creative industries takes us towards quite different objectives even though there is some continuity in the personnel involved (Stuart Cunningham, for instance, is a vehicle for that transition) (Cunningham, 2004)[14]. The move from cultural policy studies to creative industries is, among other things, a move from the nation-state – the location of regulatory and developmental interests in the culture industries – to the global market, the desired location of commercializable convergent enterprises. The beneficiary of the earlier project is the nation, the citizen and, typically, the state-subsidized cultural organization. The beneficiary of the later project is the entrepreneur, the commercial industry, and, possibly, the consumer. The move from cultural policy studies to creative industries is also, most definitively, a retreat from a commitment to the public good and its replacement by a belief in the social utility of a market outcome, reflecting the classic neo-liberal view that commercial success or 'wealth creation' for the enterprises concerned in itself constitutes a public good. Where the former was directly engaged with developing its potential as a social, political, cultural and theoretical project, the latter is primarily focused upon economic and market-development objectives as themselves facilitators of other kinds of social progress. Finally, in contrast to cultural policy studies, and while many articles have been published outlining this particular formation of the creative industries agenda, in my view, it is yet to develop a credible theoretical literature. Creative industries does have an active research agenda, and many of its research projects feed into wider debates about cultural policy and convergence culture, but as a result of its dependence upon the agendas set by commercial industries and government agencies, it tends to be more descriptive than critical in its approach.

The second narrative approaches this territory from a slightly different perspective in order to reveal other aspects of the same concerns. Within the Australian university system over the past decade or two, in a context in which the government investment in university budgets has declined from something like 80 per cent of their operating funds to less than 50 per cent, the pressure upon universities to invest in activities which will earn external funds has increased. This is a widespread trend, internationally, reflecting the rethinking of public investment in universities in most Western countries – although, significantly, much less uniformly in modernizing 'second world' nation-states. In the Australian context, at the same time as the total numbers of students have grown, funding per student has plummeted. Over this period, however, the allocation of funding to government research agencies has increased significantly, as has the number of strategic funding programmes aimed at supporting particular research areas. Although the humanities disciplines, broadly conceived[15], continue to attract the largest proportion of student enrolments across the country, they are often denied access to these strategic research funds. (For example, a five-year national research infrastructure programme charged with distributing over AUSD $500 million across the sector spent none of that money on infrastructure for the humanities, and negligible amounts on the social sciences[16].) This has knock-on effects in the overall funding environment for these disciplines, which is, in complicated ways, influenced by success in earning external research dollars. In addition, successive governments have justified their cuts to university budgets through a utilitarian and vocational rhetoric that has had the effect of undermining the principle that a university education is intrinsically valuable. Any erosion of such principled support for a university education disproportionately impacts on programmes with a liberal arts or humanities orientation; as a result, even though such programmes have continued to attract students, they have had to pay close attention to the vocational preferences of the market and to the restricted pools of strategic research funds to which they can apply. While some large, well-endowed universities have been able to protect themselves from these pressures, most universities have had to redesign their offerings to attract students at the same time as adopting highly strategic tactics in their research activities. No matter how cannily this is done, the arts and the humanities remain at the bottom of the funding food chain, collecting whatever crumbs fall off the table while the sciences are tucking in.

This concerns more than just the fields of cultural studies, creative industries, new media and so on; these pressures have had a transformative effect on the make-up of the whole of the humanities and social science research fields in Australia over the past twenty years. One of the lifelines humanities researchers have taken up is a stream of industry-based collaborative research funding (Australian Research Council Linkage Grants) which, notwithstanding the complicated issues involved in setting up partnerships and managing the intellectual property they generate, has particularly benefited researchers working on new media[17] because of their relative success in accessing industry partner funding. There is an argument, though, which suggests that the ready availability of Linkage funding has skewed research activity in these areas until now it is too far away from 'blue-sky' or curiosity-driven research and too close to industry imperatives or government agency agendas (McGuigan, 2006: 142). As a result of the pressures I have outlined, researchers seeking success in their Linkage applications have been forced to reinvent themselves so that their work is more palatable to employers and more useful to industry or government. Consequently, the QUT rebranding is far from unique in closing down whole disciplines in order to reposition its offerings in the market. Now, it is only at the large metropolitan universities, the so-called Group of Eight or 'sandstones'[18], where a comprehensive range of humanities disciplines have been maintained; everywhere else that has proven too difficult in a situation where there are a declining number of incentives to do so.

Usually, there are compelling local reasons for each strategy for survival and so they are always understandable if not necessarily inevitable. As an aggregated outcome of national funding regimes, however, this is having a devastating effect on the state of the humanities in Australia. Among the casualties are departments and offerings in foreign languages, classics, English and history. Of course, cultural studies, over its history, has defined itself in ways that have emphasized its opposition to the traditional dispositions of the humanities disciplines, and so perhaps it is not surprising that it has been among the beneficiaries of the shifts which have weakened disciplines such as English. Like some other initiatives in the so-called 'new humanities', cultural and media studies programmes are attractive to students, they are usually connected with an industry training major, and they have been one of the areas where Australian research has attracted the most international attention. To some extent, then, cultural and media studies are well equipped to survive the new environment. Nonetheless, notwithstanding cultural studies' foundational resistance to the elitism and exclusivity of the traditional humanities disciplines and therefore its positioning as a modernizing and interdisciplinary alternative to them, there remain some important continuities between the cultural studies project and aspects of the traditional humanities disciplines. What I am thinking of is a shared critical and analytic tradition that has always informed the practice of cultural studies and remains a key component of what a humanities and liberal arts education, in its various guises, can offer (Turner, 2006). This practice does not seem to have survived the shift to convergence culture.

What this second narrative emphasizes is the widespread effect of these external pressures. My primary concern is not only with the specific disciplinary casualties, although they are worrying enough. I am also concerned that the distinctiveness of a critical, analytic, academic education has been displaced by such an uncomplicatedly instrumental and training agenda. And what seems most distinctive to me about so many of the convergence culture degree programmes is their ready complicity with this new agenda; it goes well beyond the reluctant but pragmatic accommodation visible in so much of the rest of the sector.

CONCLUSION

We have seen, then, that the convergence culture degree programmes now compete with and sometimes displace generalist Arts degrees. They are also beginning to displace the cultural studies programmes that tend to reside in these generalist degrees – even though they do none of the things a cultural studies programme does. While they represent themselves as continuous with cultural studies approaches, they are not. As I noted earlier, the content of the degree programmes themselves make this abundantly clear. In the dozen or so programmes I examined in the UK and Australia, I only came across a tiny handful of course units which even mentioned cultural studies, let alone situated it as an enabling or core discipline.

The other thing I want to say about this situation is to highlight how different it is, in its very nature, to the way that cultural studies began. Cultural studies may have resisted calling itself a discipline, but it has always had the capacity to become one: it has a rich and deep intellectual tradition, it has now a history of research practices and methodologies, and it has an unfolding theoretical, political and ethical rationale that motivates its prosecution no matter what the institutional or governmental context in which it finds itself. Convergence culture has none of this. Indeed, in its most of its formations, it is simply a brand, used to position each degree programme as 'cool' and contemporary. Brands have limited life cycles and so it is reasonable to expect this one to lose its effectiveness in time – perhaps quite soon. What worries me, given the brand's claim to share an intellectual genealogy with cultural studies, is the danger that it might take cultural studies with it. Its relation to the history of cultural studies could end up being the demarcation of its vanishing point.

Convergence culture's optimistic engagement with a sector of the market it sees as innovative, alternative and democratic certainly has its share of defenders – hence the need for the reconsideration of its impact and importance. Even in that context, however, and notwithstanding the criticisms to be made, it is appropriate to acknowledge that convergence culture is an idea with its heart in the right place: it seeks empowerment for the individual, it welcomes what it sees as the democratizing potential of new media, and it is sufficiently idealistic to hope that the new media enterprises that attract their interest will achieve something more socially useful than commercial success. The criticism I have to make of those who identify with the convergence culture model is not to do with the attractiveness of their ideals. However, I think we need to consider the possibility that the shift in higher education in which I argue they are so directly implicated, when viewed from the vantage point of their origins in cultural studies, constitutes an unnecessarily comprehensive form of surrender[19]. And look at what it surrenders: a set of ethical, moral and progressive academic objectives, and an important intellectual tradition that is mature, dynamic and productive. It does this in order to cater to a market formation that has convinced them of an alignment between their interests. In my view, this alignment is exaggerated at best and spurious at worst, and we have little to gain from investing in it to the extent we have; doing so gives up on the value of an independent, critical, intellectual project. It also gives up on the value of a liberal arts and humanities degree, becoming complicit with a trend in which so many university systems seem no longer to respect what these degrees offer. I will return to the concerns I have about this in Chapter 6, but it is important to record here my view that there are aspects of the way that the convergence culture paradigm has played out which are at odds with the idea of the university as a public good, and cavalier in their disregard for the importance of a generalist academic degree that teaches critical analysis and a grasp of history across the full range of its participating disciplines.

Even though universities these days talk of themselves ceaselessly as businesses, there are many ways in which, even now and despite their best efforts, this is just not true. One of these is the extent to which the university remains a privileged and productive space for reflection, for theoretical development, for analysis and critique. Cultural studies exemplifies what possibilities can flourish within that space. My fear is that to have surrendered that space as if it no longer mattered, and for so little in terms of what we gain in return, will turn out to have been a mistake from which there will be no recovery.

NOTES

1   Cunningham (2004) maps this process in some detail.
2   This refers to the inflation of the price of tulips shortly after their introduction to Western Europe in the seventeenth century, when tulips became, briefly, the flimsy foundation for a new speculative economy.
3   I don't pretend to be an expert on this region, although it has been part of my research interest for some time now. Therefore I should acknowledge that there is a large literature on this. See the special issues of the *International Journal of Cultural Studies* (2004, 7 (1); 2006, 9 (3)) for what is largely (but not entirely) the pro-creative industries view, and then the several critiques by O'Connor (2009, in press), and O'Connor and Xin (2006), which provide more detailed evidence for the kind of argument I am making here. Further, the position I am criticizing here is similar to the position which I have characterized as 'digital optimism' in relation to the rise of alternatives to television, and the more elaborated arguments I would make against it are also similar. See Turner (2009b).
4   I would not want to exaggerate the scale of this; currently, in the UK, for instance, there are probably still a little more than half as many departments with the terms 'creative industries' or 'cultural industries' in their titles as those with 'cultural studies' in their titles. It is significant for my argument, though, that the number of the former is on the increase while the number of the latter is not, and the shifts in funding within the sector would seem to support those programmes which attract the greatest share of the market.

5 The Pew Research Centre's Internet and American Life Project's report, *Older Adults and Social Media*, written by Mary Madden (27 August 2010), found that the fastest growing demographic for social media use was those between 50 and 64 – their participation rates almost doubled (from 25 per cent to 47 per cent) in the period April 2009 to May 2010 (http://pewinternet.org/Reports/2010/Older-Adults-and-Social-Media.aspx (last accessed 16 September 2010)).

6 Why notice this? One of the interesting distinctions between the adjacent fields of communications studies and cultural studies is that until recently it was seen as virtually impossible to conceive of cultural studies being located within a business programme. While it is not unusual for communications to be housed there, cultural studies was regarded as antithetical to the commercial orientation of a business programme. That does seem to be changing – and not always for worrying reasons.

7 Not to mention what Toby Miller describes as the spectacle of those who once spent decades 'problematising creativity' now 'endorsing it' (2004: 55).

8 The content of these can vary quite widely, from the Media Studies 2.0 advanced by David Gauntlett (2007) to the 'cultural science' model proposed by John Hartley (2008). The politics of these two examples are also very different.

9 Due to the range of nomenclature used, and to the fact that while a school or department might call itself creative industries without actually offering a degree programme of that name, it is quite hard to be confident that one's search for these programmes is comprehensive. However, I have looked at all the programmes I could locate in both countries and so I am confident that they constitute at the very least a representative sample sufficient to give an idea of the major tendencies.

10 Tony Bennett's contribution to the Grossberg et al. anthology (1992) is arguably the point at which this becomes a paradigm of international significance.

11 Stuart Cunningham's (1992) *Framing Culture* was particularly controversial in its claims to replace the critical tradition in cultural studies; debates about this book and indeed what came to be called 'the policy moment', were sufficiently important to warrant the commissioning of a special issue of Australia's premier media journal, *Media Information Australia*, devoted to discussing it (Flew et al., 1994).

12 This was the UK Government's Department of Culture, Media and Sport's policy framework, *The Creative Industries Mapping Document* (1998); in this policy, there does seem to be a significant debt to the Australian government's *Creative Nation* (1994) policy even though this was very much a cultural industries rather than a creative industries approach.

13 See Justin O'Connor's (2009) extremely thoughtful and useful critique of the QUT Creative Industries research agenda.

14 It is worth making the point here that it is probably the cultural industries paradigm, particularly as it has developed in the UK, which is the next logical development from cultural policy studies; it has similar policy interests, as well as a strong and interdisciplinary intellectual foundation that connects with political economy on one side and cultural studies on the other. However, I noticed some blurring of the distinction between this tradition and the creative industries in a number of the teaching programmes I looked at in the UK. Their respective research agendas, though, still seem to me to be quite distinct and the treatment given to creative industries in Hesmondhalgh's book on the cultural industries (2007) would seem to support that view.

15 That is, if we think of this as encompassing both the traditional disciplines such as history and philosophy as well as the so-called 'new humanities', such as cultural studies, gender studies, and media studies.

16 This was the National Collaborative Research Infrastructure Strategy (NCRIS).

17 Success rates for these are more than double those for the 'basic research' programme, the Discovery grants. It is, therefore, the place for early career researchers to go, and those with a limited track record, with some hope for success. Concentrating efforts here, then, certainly increases income. For those with strong industry connections, such as the creative industries, it has proven a successful way to generate research income and some short-term employment for researchers. What it doesn't help, though, is the development of a theoretical base and an independent research agenda.

18 These are the Universities of Adelaide, Sydney, Melbourne, Queensland, Tasmania, Western Australia, Monash and New South Wales.

19 I should acknowledge that this formulation was raised in a conversation with my colleague Mark Andrejevic.

INTERNATIONALIZING CULTURAL STUDIES: FROM DIASPORA TO INDIGENEITY

5

The 2010 Cultural Crossroads conference, the biennial meeting of the international Association for Cultural Studies (ACS), was held in Hong Kong. The choice of location reflects the organization's objective of shifting the international focus of cultural studies beyond its original Anglo-American axis so that it might genuinely engage with the practice of cultural studies in non-Anglophone, non-Western locations. The intention to do this has been there from the beginning but it has been particularly evident in recent years: the 2006 conference was the first to be held outside the 'Northern European and North American centres of "academic English" cultural studies' (Morris and Wright, 2009), in Istanbul, and the 2008 conference was in Kingston, Jamaica[1]. Such choices indicate ACS's commitment to address what has been a longstanding tension within this association: the competing interests of those who come from Anglo-European or North American locations, the earliest heartlands of cultural studies, and those who do not – although that formulation should not imply that the interests and objectives of the various national groupings within these categories are necessarily homogeneous. The conflict between these two sets of interests dates back to the organization's very beginnings; its establishment was first proposed at the 2000 Crossroads conference in Birmingham and met significant resistance from, not only but in particular, participants from Latin America. While the ACS has survived this early split in the field, it has had to deal continually with the difficulties of establishing a truly inclusive international organization against the grain of the many economic, cultural and political factors which marginalize and disadvantage those who don't come from the affluent West. Even though the ACS has pursued this goal with great assiduity over recent years, nonetheless it is still true that, for some in cultural studies, the project of 'internationalization' will always require scrutiny, no matter how honourable its intentions appear to be. (Paradoxically, one of those I would identify with such a view, Kuan-Hsing Chen, plays a leading role in the Inter-Asia Cultural Studies movement, which I will discuss later in this chapter as an exemplar of successful internationalization.) On the other hand, for those who wish to act on their honourable intentions, the structural differences which bedevil the internationalization of cultural studies demand to be recognized and addressed through, for instance, explicit strategies of 'de-centring' – such as providing translation facilities for non-English speakers at conferences, subsidizing the travel and registration costs for participants from poorer countries, inviting keynote speakers from outside the hegemonic zones and so on.

This latter group are far more numerous now, indeed perhaps even the majority, than once was the case. It is worth remembering that in the early days of the project of internationalization, however, there was still another group, for whom the propagation of the Western version of cultural studies was an unproblematically 'global' movement which perfectly exemplified a pleasingly postmodern shift towards cosmopolitanism, and provided a fruitful opportunity for manifesting a theorized scepticism about the category of the nation. In one of their several contributions to what turned out to be a long-running series of debates about the internationalization of cultural studies in the mid-1990s, Jon Stratton and Ien Ang drew attention to the need to look more carefully at such an assumption:

> In all the enthusiasm currently surrounding the proliferation of cultural studies, one tends to lose sight of the fact that this presumed internationalism is hardly truly international at all. Simon

> During, working out of Australia and the editor of the recently published *Cultural Studies Reader* (which is itself a symptom of the cultural studies boom) states quite insouciantly that cultural studies has now become a 'genuinely global movement'. Yet if we look more closely at who is included in this so-called movement, we must conclude that it doesn't quite deserve the predicate 'international' let alone 'global'. (1996: 361)

I imagine it is very unlikely that Simon During would write anything like such a description now, and this points to the fact that things have changed significantly in the intervening years[2]. The field currently operates through a more sophisticated sense of how instantiated such claims have to be, and how contingent and locally grounded the practice of cultural studies has become. On the other hand, of course, and as we have seen in Chapter 2's discussion of the limits to cultural studies' institutionalization, it also highlights just how hubristic were the early claims for cultural studies' world domination.

Although it was certainly vibrantly international, the 2010 Hong Kong Crossroads conference was not, of course, a global event; a feature of these conferences in recent years has been how thoroughly located they have been. Rather than following the standard Western model of transporting the Anglo-European-American academic establishment in a particular field to do their stuff in an exotic location, the ACS conferences have offered the location the chance to do *its* stuff instead. Hence, what was most interesting about the Hong Kong conference for me was how much it was an Asian event. While there were more than respectable numbers of North American and European registrants, and while some of the keynotes and mini-plenaries were presented by names familiar to students of Western cultural studies (Tony Bennett, Larry Grossberg), many were new names (to me, at least) speaking from their own locations in Asia. This did not at all feel like a 'talking back', I should add, to a Western cultural studies establishment (and I take this to signal that we are well past this now), but rather an unselfconscious speaking from a specific place. These were scholars who had built their reputations in East Asia but were less well known outside it; some had come, however, intellectually fully formed to cultural studies, and were able to find new ways of adopting and using the insights of the field while taking them to new research sites and contexts. It has to be said, though, that in the parallel sessions where papers reported on research from Latin America and the Pacific, the work from these locations did not necessarily attract the large audiences. The practical, logistic, as well as the political, difficulties of achieving a comprehensive inclusiveness at such an event are evident here. Nonetheless, it was certainly my impression of the event, perhaps as a consequence of the intensity of the experience of the conference (the conference setting, the support and organization provided by the wonderful Lingnan students, and the vitality of Hong Kong itself), that we were witnessing something like a shift in cultural studies' geographic centre of gravity.

This may be an exaggeration and I suppose it risks implying that cultural studies can only have *one* 'centre'; perhaps, too, one might take such an impression away from any conference that was significantly localized. But it does strike me as an appropriate response to the distinctiveness and located-ness of the modes of cultural studies presently practised in Asia. I will return to this later, when I want to look more closely at the Inter-Asia Cultural Studies movement, but first I want to review some aspects of the story of how we got to this point, by talking a little about the kinds of concerns that greeted the expansion beyond the UK of what the Americans chose to call British cultural studies[3] in the 1980s and 1990s.

FROM DIASPORA TO INDIGENEITY[4]

There is a widely quoted comment, drawn from a letter to *Screen*, which dates from the early days of the internationalization of British cultural studies; Andre Frankovits reports on the 'inordinate number of left academics wandering around Australia but talking about Birmingham' (1987: 122). Mostly, this is quoted in order to highlight what is regarded as the anachronistic fetishization of the Birmingham school of cultural studies by emphasising its proponents' failure to accommodate themselves to (or indeed even to recognize) their relocation into an entirely different cultural and political space. It also highlights what is now a less widely noticed aspect of the internationalization of the British[5] invention of cultural studies – that is, its initial history as essentially a diasporic formation created by the many British cultural studies academics who fled Thatcher's Britain to Australia, Canada, New Zealand and the USA over the 1980s. This diaspora carried with it variations of the usual symptoms: nostalgia for a homeland, a deterritorialized relation to the new location, and a complex set of ongoing negotiations around the construction of cultural identities. But it had some other peculiarities as well.

For a start, it was marked by the fact that the initial 'sites of transplantation' of the British development of cultural studies 'ironically echoed the original map of British imperialism's conquests' (Morley and Ang, 1989: 136). That is, the first, and most effective, wave of migration was into Australia, Canada and the USA. Unlike most diasporic formations, though, many of the British cultural studies academics who moved into these locations were anything but deterritorialized or deracinated; on the contrary, they brought with them an assumption of their direct connection to the imperial centre that was – in most instances, at least initially – endorsed in spades by those receiving them. The Anglocentricity of the Australian practice of cultural studies in some of its earlier formations reflects this; not only were many British accents heard from the lectern at Australian cultural studies conferences (admittedly, this has never been unusual in Australian academia), but the teaching of cultural studies was also infested with readings and examples drawn from the UK. Consequently, for instance, Australian students in the 1980s were subjected to viewing grainy third-generation video copies of the British social realist TV docu-dramas *Boys from the Blackstuff* and *Days of Hope*, in order that they might follow the debates between *Screen* and the Birmingham Centre for Contemporary Cultural Studies alumni over realism and the progressive text (cf. Bennett et al., 1981). This kind of thing happened elsewhere as well – Canada, for instance, had a similar experience and the cultural authority of the British 'star' academic was used to drive the first wave of cultural studies' expansion into the USA. In Australia, it has to be said, the imperial centre may have been accorded excessive respect initially but fortunately that didn't last; by the early 1990s, the British influence had receded as local work developed and created its own distinctive international presence. In fact, Australia was one of the first locations to generate explicit critiques of the limitations inherent in accepting the Britishness of cultural studies, occasioning a rebuke from Stuart Hall in an interview with Kuan-Hsing Chen in 1996, where he chided the Australians about their 'unnecessary' desire for 'wreaking an Oedipal revenge' (Chen, 1996a: 398):

> SH: Some people, as it were, need to take their distance from a given positioning in order to win themselves intellectual space to do their work. This is a particular sensitivity in Australia. Australia has always had a sort of dependent relationship to the British and European cultural formations. In order for people practising cultural studies there to win space, they are going to adopt quite a sharp, polemical edge against certain features of what has been held up to them as a model. (401)

So the diasporic intellectual was certainly not going to have it all their own way, and as time has gone by the development of cultural studies in each location has indeed turned out to be increasingly contingent and thus increasingly indigenized. As this process gains momentum, the diasporic relation more or less disappears – or if it doesn't disappear altogether, at the very least it loses its privileges[6]. As cultural studies is taken up in Latin America and Asia from the early 1990s, there is much less evidence of the deference to the imperial centre that marks the earlier phase of expansion. To the contrary – the Inter-Asia Cultural Studies movement clearly demonstrates this and what I know about Latin American cultural studies does as well – there is an aggressive assertion of the local, national and regional determinants and articulations of what cultural studies could become.

One could take Andre Frankovits' (1987) comment as implying that the contribution of these early émigrés was largely backward-looking, nostalgically and self-importantly invoking the Birmingham of their origins. While there was certainly nothing inevitable about the influence of these diasporic British academics in their new locations, and so as not to be too 'unnecessarily Oedipal' about this, it is important to acknowledge that over time their contribution has been, and in some ways continues to be, profound. This has been in different ways and for different reasons in each instance. If we just look at one example, that of John Fiske, we can get an idea of what such a contribution did involve.

John Fiske is particularly significant because he played an important role in establishing and popularizing his variant of British cultural studies in both Australia and the USA. While he was working in Australia in the early 1980s, he took the lead role in setting up the *Australian Journal of Cultural Studies*, he deployed his significant international standing as a means of authorizing new cultural studies teaching programmes in several universities, and he brought the key cultural studies publisher Routledge into direct contact with a generation of Australian-based authors. He was a charismatic, highly provocative speaker who was skilled at popularizing the ideas of cultural studies; he was also one of the most gifted university teachers I have ever seen[7]. Like a number of other British expatriates in Australia at the time – John Tulloch, Tony Bennett, Colin Mercer, among them – Fiske seemed more institutionally optimistic and also more confident about the capacity of cultural studies to attract students than his Australian colleagues. That proved to be one important factor, among many, in the comparatively rapid institutionalization of cultural studies in Australia. In the mid-1980s, Fiske was invited to take up, first, a short-term visiting position at the University of Iowa and, then, a continuing chair at the University of Wisconsin-Madison. In a complicated series of outcomes, Fiske's move to the USA resulted in the Australian journal being taken over by Routledge, renamed *Cultural Studies*, and over time, its editorial base being transferred to the USA, where it has remained. It is now, of course, one of the leading international journals in the field. While teaching at the University of Wisconsin-Madison, which he did until 2000, Fiske was extremely influential in the development of cultural studies in America. Not only did he speak at universities all over the USA and beyond, while publishing books that were widely discussed within the field, but he also attracted some very talented graduate students who went on to become highly influential themselves. Henry Jenkins is just one of many who were taught by Fiske and who went on to play a role in shaping cultural studies in America. Regrettably, in this latter part of his academic career[8], Fiske became the standard target for attacks on cultural studies' cultural populism, and as a result, in my view, the positive benefits of his public and institutional influence have been undervalued. However, he does provide a good example (and there could be many others, Andrew Ross, say, or Tony Bennett) of the important role played by the British expatriate scholar in setting up cultural studies in English-speaking contexts outside the UK[9].

While I would argue that the British cultural studies diaspora was substantially enabling in significant ways – authorizing cultural studies as a field that had international recognition, bringing new theoretical material to these locations, brokering international networking and collaborative relationships, mentoring local scholars, and prosecuting institutional development – it didn't necessarily result in the production of an indigenized or locally inflected version of cultural studies. While Australia was quick to develop such a version, for a variety of reasons (including the character of the British diaspora there[10]), Canada took much longer but did so without such substantial involvement from British expatriates. New Zealand, despite a steady supply of British émigrés, is arguably still to do this. In all cases, however, these developments – taking place as they did within the history of a colonial relation to the former imperial power – incorporated to some extent the many myths of origins that inevitably privileged the British tradition. Indeed and as I noted in the Introduction, for some years cultural studies was almost exclusively a British formation, with minimal penetration even into the European university system. That changes most rapidly when cultural studies begins to attract attention in the USA.

The introduction of 'British cultural studies' to the American university is the point at which many of the debates about the nature and indeed the wisdom of cultural studies' internationalization gain momentum. There are two dominant stories here. One predicts that the expansion of cultural studies into the American academy would rob cultural studies of its 'critical edge' (Chen, 1996a), leading to what Pfister (1996) called a 'post-political' cultural studies. That is, disconnected from its Marxist roots in the British traditions of the humanities and social sciences, cultural studies would devolve into what would essentially be a conventionally academic, rather than a political, enterprise[11]. There seemed to be some justification for this view at the time. According to Morley and Ang, as early as 1989, a feature of the performance of American cultural studies was that 'theoretical sophistication often seem[ed] to override any sense of concrete political engagement and involvement' (1989: 135). The alacrity with which cultural studies approaches were taken up by university English departments in the USA as a means of extending their discipline's purchase on the productions of popular culture, demonstrating the viability of textual analysis as a method of dealing with such material, also tended to suggest that it would be easily incorporated by traditional disciplines, and its cultural politics neutralized. The spectre of this possibility haunted the famous 'Cultural Studies: Now and in the Future' conference at the University of Illinois,

Champaign–Urbana in 1990, and it can be tracked through the Grossberg et al. (1992) doorstopper that came out of that conference (see, in particular, the questions and answer sections where this comes up time and again).

The second story is the more interesting, in my view, and it has to do with debates about what I would prefer to call the cultural specificity of theory but what was more customarily discussed as a conflict between 'the particular' and 'the universal'. Within this story, the danger of internationalizing cultural studies was thought to lie in the de facto establishment of a body of assumptions and approaches that were held to be universal, when the overwhelming logic of a located cultural studies should be, rather, to force us to examine the particularities of the specific conjuncture we wish to understand. This contradiction proved to be a little difficult to negotiate and raised some thorny questions. If we were to privilege the particular too heavily, for instance, precisely how might we continue to think of cultural studies as a shared project? Or, to put it another way, if there is in fact *not* going to be a universalizing dimension to an internationalized cultural studies, what precisely is it that we would be internationalizing?

Stratton and Ang were among the earliest to try to think through the fact there was indeed, no matter how contradictory this might seem, an unavoidably universalizing implication to the expansion of cultural studies beyond the locations where it had originally developed. Given this, they were particularly concerned about how we might manage the politics of an expansion of cultural studies not only across borders within the West but especially between East and West. Here, they argued that it was fundamental to the cultural studies project that it find ways to resist an implicit universalism:

> it is in this resistance to universalisation that cultural studies can assert its difference from a modern discipline such as sociology, and it is in its insistence on the importance of local positioning that cultural studies exposes sociology's complicity in repressing

those aspects of the particular which cannot be subsumed under the universal. However, what is at issue is not just a question of prioritizing the particular over the universal. Just as any invocation of the universal is never innocent, any assertion of particularity also cannot go unquestioned. (Stratton and Ang, 1996: 367)

The intricacies of positioning that such a point of view generates became a major preoccupation for cultural studies through the late 1980s into the 1990s. At its worst, this was a disabling preoccupation, as the complexities of the argument required to properly interrogate how the particular might be constructed in any one instance were potentially paralysing. The discussion of what was at the time referred to as one's 'speaking position' had a tendency to spiral regressively into an essentialist version of identity politics that has to some extent now, thankfully, receded.

Yet, at the time, it did seem like these were key questions to be explored. I should acknowledge that I played a vigorous part in these debates myself, arguing for the cultural specificity of Australian cultural studies and taking on the British tradition as my straw man, as Hall suggests, in order to establish points of difference (Turner, 1992). Stratton and Ang describe me, perhaps exaggerating a little, as 'one of the most vocal resenters of the Anglo-American hegemony in "international" cultural studies and the centrality of British cultural studies in it' (1996: 379). It was, in fact, relatively typical for the Australian variant of cultural studies to take on the task of arguing that cultural studies needed to 'work' for the margins as well as for the centres, and my line on this was no different: 'cultural studies', I argued 'has a lot to gain from the margins, and it should do its best to investigate the ways in which their specific conditions demand the modification of explanations generated elsewhere'(Turner, 1992: 641). Characteristic of the way arguments were being made at that time, I suggested that such considerations needed to be built into the expansion of the cultural studies project in order to 'provide a hedge against the development of a new universalism' (641). One can see from the way Stratton and Ang interrogate this position in their own discussion, that these were still hotly contested debates. Also hotly contested was any suggestion that we might resolve this debate through the adoption of an 'area studies' style of multidisciplinary tolerance or pluralism, on the one hand, or a re-inscription of 'the national' on the other. As Stratton and Ang put it:

> We think that it is through the elaboration of such positions that the international *rendez-vous* of cultural studies practitioners can attempt to problematize the universalisms of existing core/periphery relations, on the one hand, and avoid degenerating into a polite but ultimately indifferent conversation between particularist, mutually exclusive nationals, on the other (1996: 385).

However you characterize the contradictions (Paul Willemen has described this as the choice between being 'cravenly multicultural or politely post-colonial' (2010: 223)), the possibility of an international cultural studies becomes a complex one, its objective to find ways to acknowledge differences without ceasing to make them matter.

As Ang and Stratton were to demonstrate, this is easier said than done. A slightly later piece developing their arguments for what they called a 'critical transnationalism' in cultural studies, appearing in a special issue of *Cultural Studies* (10:1, 1996) devoted to 'controversies in cultural studies', provoked a strenuous rejoinder from Kuan-Hsing Chen (the response was actually longer than the original essay). Chen accused Ang and Stratton of an implicit nationalism, a position he criticized from the point of view of his preferred alternative – an explicitly anti-imperialist regionalism (1996c). Ang and Stratton responded in turn – all of this in one issue of the journal – by accusing Chen of essentializing nationalism and oversimplifying its diverse capacities, formations and functions. They restated their interest in understanding how the politics of nationalism can play out in different political and cultural contexts and argued that it is wrong to assume in advance that the national, or indeed the nation-state, will always serve the same ideological functions and political interests – so that 'any engagement with the nation-state' at all is 'necessarily complicit with "the bad guys"' (Ang and Stratton, 1996c: 72).

Kuan-Hsing Chen has been among the most polemical and uncompromising contributors on this topic, over many years; he was also one of the driving forces behind the development of the Inter-Asia Cultural Studies movement and, with Chua Beng-Huat, he is a founding co-editor of the Routledge journal *Inter-Asia Cultural Studies*. He is also the interlocutor with Stuart Hall in two interviews in a collection Chen co-edited with David Morley and which is focused on Hall's work (1996a,b). In the first of these interviews, which deals specifically with the internationalization of cultural studies, one of Chen's questions takes us back to what I discussed a little earlier in this section, the 'story' of concerns about cultural studies' expansion into America and the subsequent danger of the field losing its mythic 'political edge':

> KHC: This is a problem in so far as it seems that the internationalization of cultural studies has somehow tended to undermine its political edge. What emerged in the 'Trajectories' conference [held in Taipei in 1992, and the beginning of the Inter-Asia movement] was a concern with that, and thus an attempt to say what is or what is not cultural studies, in order to retain that political edge. We understand very well that, especially in the American context, in the process of institutionalization in the academy, cultural studies can easily lose that 'edge'. (Chen, 1996a: 395)

Hall is reluctant to adopt the position that Chen offers him here; to the contrary, he declines to take on the task of policing cultural studies boundaries by defending an 'originary' position, 'to pronounce what British cultural studies was and was not' (Chen, 1996a: 395). He does respond, however, to the question about American cultural studies by providing a nuanced reading of the specificity of cultural studies as it develops in the USA, and its relation to the local political, cultural and academic contexts.

Another of Hall's comments in this interview returns us to the second story I mentioned, the problem of the universal and the particular. Early in his conversation with Chen, Hall chooses the metaphor of translation to describe how British cultural studies might be made useful in locations other than Britain:

> What interests me about this is that, everywhere, cultural studies is going through this process of re-translation. It's going through the process of re-translation wherever it is being taken up, in the United States, Australia, Canada, particularly. Each of these places is involved in its own re-translation. (Chen, 1996a: 393)

When challenged on the choice of this metaphor by Chen, Hall places 'translation' in 'quotation marks because it doesn't mean that there is an original from which the "translation" is a copy' (393). Chen won't accept this qualification as the metaphor still implicitly endows the British origins of cultural studies with the determining force of the original language, when in fact, he suggests, 'the new configurations seem to have left the "originary" movement of cultural studies behind, with 'everything now flowing in different directions'. Indeed, he says provocatively, '"British" cultural studies is no longer needed' (394). Hall patiently accepts this comment but makes the important (and accurate) historical point that while he understands 'declarations of independence of that kind', they nonetheless 'misrepresent what new conjunctions are really about – they are never absolute ruptures, total breaks' (Chen, 1996a: 394).

Documenting examples of this kind of exchange over the 1990s could fill a book on its own. The point I want to make from this brief excursion into them is that, 15 years on, some of the heat has gone out of these debates, largely because of the way that cultural studies has just gone ahead and established itself in particular ways in all kinds of places. A way of making this point might be to draw a comparison between the 1996 issue of *Cultural Studies* (10:1) which dealt with internationalization as its major 'controversy in cultural studies', and the 2009 (23 (5–6)) issue on 'transnationalism and cultural studies'. The 1996 issue dealt with internationalization through a largely unlocated (that is, universalizing) theoretical debate about positionality; the 2009 issue was devoted to examples of the practice of cultural studies that presented transnational, comparative and localized research. None of its research locations came from the Anglo-American 'centre'. The one article in the 2009 issue which does devote itself to a theoretical discussion of internationalization makes the point that, for some nationalities, there was never the option of *not* internationalizing; for the author, Raka Shome, as an Indian woman working in the USA, 'there was nothing that was not already 'international' in [her] relation to cultural studies' (2009: 702). From Shome's point of view, however, what had changed in the actual practice of cultural studies, what was 'new about many of the efforts at internationalization' currently in play, was 'the *equality* of imagination, recognition, and speaking positions across borders and boundaries that are now being demanded' (703, emphasis in original). This issue of *Cultural Studies* reveals – and there are of course many other locations where the same point is also illustrated – that we have indeed moved on from that 1990s debate over universalism. In my opinion, this is because the theoretical debate has been overtaken by changes in practice. There is now a raft of indigenous formations of cultural studies in place, across the East as well as the West. They are not simply translations of utterances from elsewhere, and they are not necessarily national in their location – they may well be regional or geo-linguistic (so, cultural studies in Asia might be an instance of the former and Latin American cultural studies an instance of the latter). Questions about the role that the nation may or not play seem to have receded as the central focus of debate while each of these varied formations of cultural studies are grounded in highly specific complexes of local, national or regional conditions.

Indeed, I think it is possible to talk about the diverse – local, national, regional or transnational – practices of cultural studies as indications that cultural studies is settling into a new, perhaps secondary but nonetheless important, role as a widely disseminated intellectual, theoretical and methodological resource which enables intellectual movements that are already under way to accomplish specific kinds of objectives. Hence Sonia E. Alvarez et al.'s (at the time of writing, unpublished) discussion of the de-centring of Latin-American Studies, which notes the controversial but significant role of cultural studies in that process[12]. Alvarez et al. describe the context for Latin American humanities scholars in general as one which has long maintained an intellectual tradition that trains its scholars 'to draw political consequences from their research'. This, Alvarez and her co-writers argue, has been the 'natural order of things' in twentieth-century Latin America and involves 'a commitment to actively fashioning our scholarship to advance a specific political "good" (human rights, gender equality, anti-racist struggle, and so forth)':

> This is more complicated, because there is no guarantee that the actions involved will all be consistent with the values and priorities of the academic community in question. While acknowledging the absence of such guarantees, scholars still need to make these connections and to announce them explicitly, for two reasons: they highlight a vital engagement with the world, which always has been a great strength of Latin American Studies; and, making these connections explicit opens greater possibilities for productive and clarifying debate. (2010: np)

At its most politically engaged, I would suggest, cultural studies is in accord with this tradition and so it is not surprising that it has exerted an influence upon it. Far from demonstrating the legitimacy of those 1990s' concerns about internationalization blunting cultural studies' political edge, I suspect that it is precisely the politics of cultural studies that makes it attractive to this particular community of scholars.

Also worth noting here is what I regard as a significant shift in how scholars have been thinking about the practice of cultural studies since the 1990s, in many of the places where it occurs. What I have in mind is a shift towards (and I *mean* 'towards') the identification of what we do as research rather than as either scholarship or theory. There are, of course, significant institutional or policy factors implicated here that affect far more than the practice of cultural studies: university funding regimes, changes in the positioning of the humanities and liberal arts within these regimes, as well as a neoliberal tendency towards either medical-izing or commercializing the preferred models of research practice – especially in state-funded university systems. While these developments have worked against our interests in many ways, instrumentalizing much of what we do in our teaching as well as our research and increasing the difficulty of prosecuting the more critical agendas of the field, I think that there are some benefits to have come from this change in the identification of cultural studies practice. For a start, it has helped to move us away (or perhaps recognizes that we have already moved away) from the obsessive interrogation of speaking position that filled so many Q&A periods in cultural studies conferences. More importantly, there is evidence that it has facilitated the establishment of a more engaged and grounded model of cultural studies practice that reduces the inclination towards a generalized universalism, on the one hand, while also giving real substance to our focus on the particular, on the other hand. Some might see this as the normalization of a conjunctural approach to cultural studies research. What is, in effect, a consequence of the professionalization and institutionalization of the field, has made these earlier debates less difficult to navigate than when they were almost entirely contained within performances of the scholarship of position.

All of that said, it remains difficult in practice for an internationalizing cultural studies to manage what Stuart Hall has described as the translation of cultural studies into new formations in a manner which ensures that these new variants are recognized and understood in their own terms. Problems of *actual* translation – that is between different languages – remain as significant barriers to the sharing of knowledges and analysis, even when they are dealing with the same thing (such as, for instance, non-Anglophone television[13]). What actually gets said is tricky too. As critical mass develops in new areas – Asia is one, Latin America is another – there is the question of how to manage a conversation between this community and some of the longer-established communities without simply restarting the standard debates about Eurocentrism, colonization and the dominance of the West. Perhaps it works best if there are mediating figures able to see both perspectives and thus help that conversation along; the role that Meaghan Morris, for instance, has played in the Inter-Asia Cultural Studies collective. However, once we are able to look at the nature of these various located practices of cultural studies in their own terms, it is a little easier to understand what a cultural studies with indigenous roots – that is, with its origins in the cultures it examines – might look like. So, let's do that briefly now.

INTER-ASIA CULTURAL STUDIES

Even as debates about universalism and particularism were flourishing in Anglo-American contexts over the 1990s, the practice of cultural studies had already migrated into non-Anglo locations where the Britishness of cultural studies was not taken for granted, nor even necessarily embraced or accepted. The beginnings of the Inter-Asia Cultural Studies (IACS) collective, for instance, can be traced back to the 1992 'Trajectories' conference in Taipei. That conference was the first in what was to become a series of IACS conferences as the group was formalized and institutionalized in various ways over the next decade or so; a professional association for Inter-Asia Cultural Studies was established in 2005. Over that period, a highly distinctive community of scholars has developed with a mix of activist and academic interests, across many nations, ethnicities, cultures and languages (including India, China, Indonesia, Taiwan, Korea, Japan, Malaysia, Singapore and Hong Kong). Based on the conviction that they needed to work from their Asian location, and thinking of that location as a methodologically crucial aspect of what they did, these scholars took a circumspect view of what the Western traditions of cultural studies had to offer. Their concerns were drawn from their own historical and political situation. Many of them had trained in the region, and some had lived through quite dramatic social and political change from which much of their professional work gained its significance:

> This is the generation who does intellectual work with the imagination (in all senses of the word) that their work, embedded in and connected directly with the society one lives in, has larger concerns and impacts; therefore, one thinks and works beyond the boundary of the academic institutions, as well as self-interest. (Chen, 2010: np)

There was never much likelihood that the take-up of cultural studies by these academics was going to result in the loss of its 'critical edge'.

I should acknowledge that the presence of this movement only gradually came to my attention. My academic networks, for the first 20 years of my career, were primarily Anglo-American, and it is not until the 1990s that I had any substantive connection with cultural studies scholars in Asia. I think it is significant, however, that over the past 10 years in particular the majority of my international activities have been in Asia. I have attended many conferences in the region, connected with many Asian-based scholars, and supervised many students from the region as well. Since 2006, I have been working on a large international project on post-broadcast television which includes Hong Kong, China, Taiwan and Singapore. I do not speak Mandarin, but my guide through Chinese language television and the cultures which produce it, Jinna Tay, does. She collaborated with me on this part of the project and taught me a great deal about the region, its media, and about the work going on there in media and cultural studies. My experience, and its chronological trajectory, is representative,

I believe, of a growing pattern of Western interest in and genuine collaboration with Asian-based scholars and intellectuals[14]. There is a significant cohort of young Australian cultural studies researchers working on Asian material with locally based colleagues[15]; at the Hong Kong Crossroads conference, there were more than 100 registrants from Australia, the largest number ever. So, while I can't claim any special personal relationship with the Inter-Asia movement itself, the emergence of an Asian-based community of cultural studies scholars is something that I have witnessed directly.

The establishment of the journal *Inter-Asia Cultural Studies* in 2000 (it was launched at the Birmingham Crossroads conference), was an important step in presenting this community to a wider international audience. The context was framed by the 1980s enthusiasm for 'the rise of Asia', which held the promise of new opportunities for the region, but which was also prosecuted through what some regarded as a worrying 'triumphalism':

> Since the 1980s, a pervasive rhetoric of the 'rise of Asia' has come to mean more than the concentrated flow of capital into and out of the region; it has come to constitute a structure of feeling that is ubiquitous, yet ambiguously felt, throughout Asia. Historically, this feeling of the 'rise of Asia' is complicated by the region's colonial past. While Asia's political, cultural and economic position in the global system will continue to fluctuate, there is a need to question and critique the rhetorical unities of both the 'rise' and 'of Asia'. Wealth and resources are unevenly distributed and there is no cultural or linguistic unity in this imaginary space called Asia. On the other hand, no matter whether there are common experiences shared by sub-regional histories, there is an urgent need for forging political links across these sub-regions. Hence, 'Inter-Asia' cultural studies. (*Inter-Asia Cultural Studies*, 2000: 5)

If cultural studies was claimed as a potential force for decolonization (Chen, 1998), the journal was established as a means of mobilizing that potential. According to its founding editors, Kuan-Hsing Chen and Chua Beng-Huat, the journal set out to 'contribute to the integration of an imagined Asia at the level of knowledge production' through generating critical work 'in and out of Asia and beyond', linking and facilitating dialogues between the various 'critical circles' within Asia and beyond, and providing a platform 'on which academic and movement intellectual work' might intersect (2007: 1). In their introduction to the *Inter-Asia Cultural Studies Reader* (2007), Kuan-Hsing Chen and Chua Beng-Huat admit that the last of these objectives remains to be met, but their success with the first two has been significant. From the beginning, the journal filled a major gap by making intellectual work produced in Asia available in English, opening up new conversations within the region as well as between the region and the English-speaking zones of cultural studies, and making a serious and sustained effort to deal with the problem of translation – not only between Asian languages and English, but among the Asian languages themselves[16]. It had other issues to address as well:

> It is not an exaggeration to say that before *IACS*, scholars and cultural workers in the region had minimal contacts with each other, not to mention any substantive comparative and associative exchanges. As indicative of the western cultural hegemony and the Cold War structure, most intellectuals would matriculate in North America or Europe, learn the most sophisticated theory and methodology, return to his/her home country to propagate 'western' learning. Scholars from Japan, India, the Philippines, Hong Kong, S. Korea, Taiwan, Malaysia, Singapore etc would seek greater affinity and affiliations, with their western counterparts than among themselves. (Ching, 2010: 185)

Inter-Asia Cultural Studies, says Ching, changed all that by providing a regional focus and an outlet for 'alternative modes of inquiry' fostering 'diaological engagement across the region' and 'prioritizing' a focus on 'inter-Asia cultures and politics' (185). Contributors to the tenth anniversary special issue agreed that the journal had achieved its central aim of 'shifting the geographies of knowledge' (Budianta, 2010).

The context for Inter-Asia is not just geographically distinctive. Reading through the issues of the journal, one is also struck by the centrality of a deep history of colonization and imperialism; it is not unusual for analyses of current conjunctures to reach back into the nineteenth century to uncover the seeds of the contemporary situation. Given the continuing presence of that history, the repressive role so often played by the state, and the violence that has so often accompanied both, one can understand the vehemence with which the nation-state is rejected as an appropriate unit of analysis[17]. The project of constructing 'Asia' as the location for their work does make its own sense – the aspiration to build coherence for academic and political activity across national borders and within the region seems to be, at least partly, the consequence of the need to work around the nation-state. It is fraught with difficulties, though, and this is reflected in the regularity with which we read articles dealing with the theorization of 'Asia', as a place, as a history, as a location for the development of cultural studies. What one also notices is that *this* – the question of Asia – is the primary ground for theoretical debate among the Inter-Asia community – not cultural studies as a disciplinary formation, and certainly not their relation to Western traditions of cultural studies. Far from vigorously engaging with the Western universalism/particularism debate in order to defend their own version of particularism, it is striking how often contributors to the journal just ignore Western cultural studies – or perhaps more accurately they take it for granted as one of the conditions within which they work but which no longer demands specification. Recalling Chen's comment to Stuart Hall that British cultural studies is no longer needed, its virtual invisibility in the pages of *Inter-Asia Cultural Studies* would seem to reinforce this claim[18].

Also among the distinctive characteristics of the Inter-Asia project is its decision to construct its work as the product of a multi-lingual, transnational, geographical region. It does this, perhaps a little paradoxically, by privileging the importance of the local. As I said, it is hardly surprising that the movement is especially suspicious of constructions of nationalism and its supporting discourses. But it is a little surprising to see how categorically what is after all a prime example of the successful internationalization of cultural studies designates the idea of the local as its reference point. Perhaps more explicitly and programmatically than any other of the indigenized cultural studies examples I can think of, IACS is the most resolutely opposed to the very idea of the nation-state and the most committed to the centrality of the local. Reflecting on this in his address on the occasion of the tenth anniversary of the journal's existence, Chen put it like this:

> Very early on, in 2001, during the editorial meeting in Beijing, a consensus was reached to commit ourselves to the priority of the local (not in the narrow sense, but in the wider sense, sometimes to mean the Asia region as a site of the local). The resulting editorial policy has been that the journal is to publish work which addresses problems internal to the local formation; deploying abstract conceptual apparatus from the outside to impose on the local is not our intellectual agenda. (2010: np)

The second half of that last sentence is a reasonably accurate description of what constitutes a lot of cultural studies writing elsewhere and it serves to highlight the existence of contrasting ways of producing knowledge. This is reinforced when one looks at what *Inter-Asia Cultural Studies* produces knowledge *about*. When one turns to the *Inter-Asia Cultural Studies Reader* (Chen and Chua, 2007), organized as it is around thematic sections in a classic Routledge manner, some of the contrasts leap off the page: for instance, there are sections on 'state violence' and 'Americanism', reflecting the reality of the kinds of issues with which cultural studies under authoritarian political regimes, or working against successive waves of colonization, has had to engage[19].

So, why do I offer IACS as an example of the move from the diasporic to the indigenous? The Inter-Asia collective is so specific, so little indebted to the diasporic roots that have been so important to the spread of cultural studies elsewhere, so distinctive in the work that it does, and so embedded in its particular political histories – and yet so directly enabled by the insights and methods that have developed over the history of cultural studies – that it provides a fascinating instance of how a field of study, even one with such strong hegemonic ties back to its origins in the West, can morph so substantially into the shape required by the context in which it is to be put to work. Dealing with these scholars one is aware of the existence of commonalities and of crucial differences; agreement cannot be taken for granted but nonetheless seems possible. It doesn't quite turn out to be the kind of 'transnational' cultural studies Ang and Stratton examined; it is not merely a distinctive iteration of something else. What it is, though, is a convincingly, multiply indigenized, regional method that thinks of its sphere of interest as being rooted, first and foremost, in the local. Far from producing a merely provincial mode of cultural studies, or becoming a 'generalist precursor of a series of national cultural studies publications' (Willemen, 2010: 221), it may have something to teach the rest of us about how to do work that matters.

CONCLUSION

Of course, the emergence of Inter-Asia is just one example of a localized but transnational formation of cultural studies, and it perhaps assumes greater significance by being located against the background of a successful international conference in Asia. It is as well not to claim too much for this example. Notwithstanding IACS's achievements, the core contradiction of working both locally and internationally remains unresolved, and at the level of the practice of cultural studies it is likely to remain that way. It is, then, a contradiction that needs to be continually and explicitly managed. We must continue to ask the questions those working in cultural studies outside the Anglo-American zones have been posing for a long time: how easy is it, to write about the local and offer that work to an international readership? How interested are publishers in work from outside the British cultural studies diaspora? What is it like, presenting work about your own location to conferences outside your own country or region? Does anyone come to hear it? When you participate in them, do conferences that present themselves as international actually deliver, in terms of genuinely prosecuting international interests? And, more broadly, does the experience of practicing cultural studies, in most places today, manifest – on the one hand – a genuinely inclusive transnationalism and – on the other hand – an uncomplicated confidence in indigeneity?

Of course, the answers to these questions will not be generic; they will depend upon which example of local work, which conference, which aspects of the practice of cultural studies we are talking about at the time. But, at present and in general in cultural studies, we know that, most of the time, someone presenting work coming from a research project on the Philippines will continue to report fewer attendees at their paper than the numbers attending papers on research topics located in or generated from the USA. The hegemony of a cultural studies 'mainstream' has not gone away. Nonetheless, I think we can say that the range of possibilities for a positive answer to at least some of the questions asked above has begun to widen. There are promising indications, even in the listings of individual titles and new series in publishers' catalogues, that there is increasing interest in publishing work from non-Western locations. If we look at how this work is taken up once it is published, it is clear that it is now more easily integrated into what has become a widening frame of reference for cultural studies research. And I would regard the rise of Asian cultural studies – and not only that which is represented by the Inter-Asia movement – as heading towards an 'inclusive transnationality and a confident indigeneity'.

There are some very positive stories to tell about the internationalization of cultural studies. If we look specifically at research activity, rather than teaching (and as we saw in Chapter

3, that is a whole other story), the evidence of the past decade or so of an international, transnational and indigenizing cultural studies suggests that the dispersal and reformation of cultural studies in various locations and contexts has not at all produced the results that were once so widely predicted – solidifying its practice into a rigid or overly standardized disciplinary model, or stripping cultural studies of its politics. Rather, the internationalization of cultural studies in recent years, while by no means a process that has achieved all its goals, seems to have been, on balance, an enabling process that has generated new kinds of work, new applications, new theoretical developments, and – most importantly of all – greater access to an enriched field of argument and research. Johan Fornas, in his contribution to the tenth anniversary issue of *Inter-Asia Cultural Studies*, where he is speaking on behalf of European and Nordic formations of cultural studies, talks about the Inter-Asia movement as an example of what he sees as an 'emerging *glocal* field of cultural studies' 'with an open range of globally interconnected but locally anchored and specific practices of doing boundary-crossing and critical cultural research' (2010: 214 [emphasis in the original]). This is not dissimilar to the manner in which Morley and Ang envisaged a transnational future for cultural studies, way back in 1989, as they emphasized the important role of the local context in determining what the practice of cultural studies might become:

> In other words, the place and relevance of cultural studies varies from context to context, and has to be related to the specific character of local forms of political and intellectual discourse on culture. In our view, it is the context-dependence of cultural studies which we need to keep in mind, and indeed reinforce, if we are to resist tendencies towards the development of orthodoxies and the temptations of a codified vocabulary-tendencies which may be the less desirable effects of internationalization. (136)

This may have been an aspirational statement then, but it is very close to describing how things have worked out since. This is not a settled condition, however, and it is noticeable that the momentum seems to have shifted from one context to another. Fornas puts it this way:

> English-speaking branches still have a hegemonic position in this field, reflecting the persistent US dominance in economy, politics and media culture, but also the key historical role played by British–American cultural studies in giving impetus to forming this research field from the start, as well as the function of English as a *lingua franca* in the academy at large. However, certain problems and forms of backlash have for some time hampered the continued consolidation of cultural studies in the UK and the USA, while there seems recently to have been more success in other parts of the world, including Latin America, East Asia and also the Nordic countries of Europe. (2010: 214)

Now, I am aware that this is still a highly complicated set of debates, and one's perspective on this issue depends upon the position from which one is viewing it. My account may look like it has its own contextual blinkers that have obscured certain important features, and it seems inevitable – when focusing on the practice of cultural studies – that one should fall victim to this from time to time. However, and even though there are indeed many places where cultural studies is in a precarious position – with low levels of institutional presence, declining enrolments, minimal research funding, snide campaigns in the local press (interestingly, both elitist and populist), worrying shifts in higher education policy, and so on – it is the way that the practice of cultural studies has been adopted and transformed within particular locations that is among the most exciting aspects of its recent histories.

Realistically, we have to acknowledge that most of the drivers to this process are out of the control of cultural studies. The institutional histories of cultural studies are enclosed within the larger histories of the volatile world of higher education funding, and the changing place of the humanities and the social sciences in that world. As I write this, the implementation of aspects of the Browne report (2010) has sent shock waves through the arts and humanities programmes in the UK. As noted earlier, this report described an education in these disciplines as inappropriate for public investment. In the USA, as the effects of the global financial crisis continue to bite, universities have closed a range of programmes in the liberal arts and humanities: including interdisciplinary programmes such as communications, gender studies and cultural studies. Just as I argued earlier that the strategic directions of higher education policy in Australia in the 1980s actually assisted the development of cultural studies programmes, the current wave of budget cuts carries the risk of producing drastically negative effects on these programmes in the UK and the USA. On the other hand, we are seeing massive investment in higher education in Asia – and the liberal arts and humanities are definitely part of that process. Ironically, it seems that while democratic Western governments are disinvesting in these disciplines in favour of an instrumentalist and utilitarian approach to higher education, authoritarian Eastern governments are reasserting their importance as one of the paths towards modernity.

The vagaries of higher education policy are also among the factors responsible for what I described as a gradual shift towards approaching cultural studies as a field of research. The design of research support programmes around project funding, despite the relatively poor fit between humanities and medical models of research, has encouraged particular kinds of behaviour: project-based research, a stronger empirical element, and a greater focus on the aims and objectives of the specific project rather than upon the more contingent and unpredictable outcomes of the practice of critique – or the universalizing aims of cultural theory. There are both good and bad things about such a regime, of course, and it is worth remembering that a regime into which humanities disciplines do not easily fit will not easily serve their interests. And there are plenty of locations where such regimes operate with political objectives in mind; the funding of research is rarely organized so that it is entirely value-free, or without some strategic strings attached, no matter how high-minded the supporting rhetoric. Assessing the effects of this repositioning of the practice of cultural studies is not a simple matter, then.

Cultural studies, just like any other discipline or interdiscipline, is unable to control or even much influence the structural and political conditions within which it must operate. The state does that. What is striking, and encouraging, is how mobile and adaptable cultural studies has proven to be across such a wide range of these conditions. What is also striking is that its approaches have continued to prove to be just plain useful, even when they have travelled far beyond the contexts within which they were originally developed. That remains the lesson I learnt from the students from Lingnan University I mentioned in Chapter 3. If this pattern continues, the future(s) for cultural studies may be closely related to these two attributes: its mobility and its utility. Cultural studies has proven to be an adaptable and resourceful traveller.

NOTES

1   See the short discussion of the issue of transnationalism within the ACS in Meaghan Morris and Handel Wright's introduction to their special issue of *Cultural Studies* (2009)

2   To be fair, During was hardly alone in making such comments. Stuart Hall, for instance, in the Chen interview, describes the internationalization of cultural studies as a process of being 'globalized' (Chen, 1996a: 393).

3   I first came across this nomenclature when I was asked to write a book introducing cultural studies to the American market at the end of the 1980s (*British Cultural Studies: An Introduction*). While I was not entirely comfortable with the label, and thus spent the first few pages of the book explaining why I used it, nonetheless it was perfectly clear that it was a widely accepted descriptor for this body of work in the USA. As it turned out, my American publisher, Unwin Hyman, sold out to Harper Collins, who sold the list to Routledge, first in the USA and then in the UK, so the book written specifically for the American market eventually found itself roundly criticized in the British market for adopting the American nomenclature for cultural studies.

4 Just to be clear: I am using this word here in its broadest sense, to invoke forms of identity and locality rather than to reference the participation of, say, First Peoples or indigenous communities. That kind of participation, it has to be said, is as rare in cultural studies as it is in most humanities disciplines in the West.

5 By phrasing it like this, I want to acknowledge the need to leave room for other versions of the history of cultural studies; the work of James Carey (1989) in the USA, for instance, both overlaps with and differentiates itself from the British cultural studies formation. It is clear, too, that many of the current generation of cultural studies scholars in Asia did their training in the USA, often well before the 'British invasion', and with American-based scholars who made their own distinctive contribution to the development of the field.

6 An important exception to this is the formation of creative industries programmes in Australia that I talked about in the previous chapter. This has interestingly replicated the history of the export of British cultural studies. It has taken up a structural model from the Blair government's creative industries policy framework, and largely prosecuted it by flying in British academics and popularizing 'futurists' such as Charles Leadbetter to present a set of arguments that are almost entirely grounded in the UK context. They have been able to offer many of these visitors to government and industry as authoritative informants about international policy trends and this has been an important means of building credibility for the approach and for the institutions concerned. Nonetheless, as was the case in the teaching of *Screen* theory, the academic project of the creative industries largely depends upon its British content (Hartley, 2009a). So, the UK's creative cities policy and, say, the urban renewal of Sheffield becomes the new *Boys from the Blackstuff*.

7 I taught with John Fiske in the early 1980s, when we were both at the Western Australian Institute of Technology, later to be called Curtin University. I collaborated with him on writing a popularizing cultural studies approach to the analysis of Australian popular culture (Fiske et al., *Myths of Oz: Reading Australian Popular Culture*, 1987). An important mentor, personally, he played a significant part in developing my interest in cultural studies by introducing me to the Open University readers in popular culture that collected some of the foundational materials for British cultural studies.

8 Fiske retired in 2000 to run an antiques business in New England. While Fiske spoke at a conference at Madison in 2010 which celebrated

his intellectual legacy, he has not played a role in the academy since his retirement.

9   Fiske's reputation was always less substantial in the UK than elsewhere.

10 Some of the British expatriates were highly committed to building institutions with a strong local or national focus; Tony Bennett's Key Centre for Cultural and Media Policy at Griffith University is the prime example of this.

11 There are many locations for these arguments as they were regular inclusions in the numerous edited collections and readers that came out over the 1990s, such as John Storey's *What is Cultural Studies?* (1996). A good example from that volume is Alan O'Connor's 'The problem of cultural studies' (1996).

12 I encountered this as a keynote presentation by Arturo Arias to the Australian Iberian and Latin American Studies Association conference in Canberra, July, 2010. Arturo Arias was kind enough to provide me with a copy of the paper, which will form the introduction to a co-edited volume on decentring Latin American studies.

13 Alvarez et al. describe a situation where the influence of cultural studies has been sufficiently profound that some sections of the Latin American studies community have described it as 'a takeover', and as displacing some earlier disciplinary foundations.

14 In my own case, when embarking on a transnational television research project, I needed to recruit researchers who spoke Spanish or Mandarin, and who had a research background in cultural, media or television studies. While I was fortunate in being able to appoint wonderful colleagues to these positions, they were not drawn from a large field of applicants.

15 The Australian component of this is a large one, but it would also include the work being done by US-based Andrew Ross in Shanghai, or by John Storey (UK) in various parts of China.

16 Examples of such collaborations include those involving Larissa Hjorth (working in Korea) and Fran Martin and Audrey Yue (working in Taiwan).

17 Perhaps the most intractable practical obstacle to this kind of transnational intellectual exchange is the problem of translation – not in the metaphoric sense I quoted Stuart Hall using it earlier, but in the conventional sense of translating between languages. Asia is of course not a homogeneous entity; even though the citizens of its nation-states may have many common interests, the differences of language and

culture are in some cases enormous. The IACS collective was committed to providing translations during IACS conferences to include local audiences as much as possible. The lengths the IACS has gone to in the attempt to achieve this aim are extraordinary. At the 1998 Taipei conference IACS used a 'guerrilla radio station' to set up channels in Chinese, Korean, Japanese and English, and asked participants to bring shortwave radios with them; friends with translation ability did voluntary work to provide the translations. In 2000, at Fukuoka, there was continuous translation as papers were presented, a strategy that has been used frequently elsewhere, but which has the downside of effectively doubling the amount of time taken up by each presentation. In 2005, at Seoul, IACS purchased portable radio receivers to enable translations to happen. By 2007, in Shanghai, the sheer size of the event defeated it, raising questions about how to find new ways of unseating English as the default language. These questions continue to dog the project of creating a community of cultural studies scholars in the region. Of course, this problem is not unique to cultural studies nor to the Asian region, but Inter-Asia has consistently tried to overcome it there particularly through using the network of Asian-based journals the association set up to translate local work for an international readership.

18 I should acknowledge that I have quite significant theoretical differences with some of the approaches I read in *Inter-Asia Cultural Studies*, and in particular these cohere around the role of the nation-state and the function of constructions of nationalism.

19 There is a notable exception to that observation, though; at least one British cultural studies orthodoxy still survives at the heart of the Inter-Asia project – the resistance to institutionalization. Even as they establish their institutions – their research centres, their university programmes, their departments of cultural studies, their journal network and their professional associations – there is still recourse to rehearsing the old concerns about the dangers of institutionalism. Chen raised them in his interview with Hall on internationalization, and 15 years later when the *Inter-Asia Cultural Studies* published its tenth anniversary issue, it carried an extraordinary contribution warning, once again, of the dangers ahead for the journal as it becomes more successful, more comfortably embedded into the professional academy, an institution in its own right (Willemen, 2010: 222). As we have seen earlier in this book, there are competing views on this issue, but to graft it on to the IACS movement seems particularly odd when it has such a strong political base.

20 They have engaged with these circumstances in distinctive ways, ways not often explored by cultural studies elsewhere. An example of this would be the comparatively high level of engagement with school education. I am thinking here of the work of Stephen Chan Ching-kiu and Hui Po-Keung, for instance, which was reported in a session at the 2010 Crossroads, and involves the development of liberal studies curricula for secondary schools in Hong Kong. Meaghan Morris mentions a raft of other instances in India, China and Korea, among other locations, in her discussion of *Inter-Asia* and education (2010: 161), indicating that the scale and focus of this work is probably unparalleled in the West. A fundamental interest in education is also evident in, again, the relatively unusual focus on the teaching of cultural studies – something I mentioned in Chapter 3, as a particular feature of Inter-Asia cultural studies, which resulted in its devoting a special issue of *Inter-Asia Cultural Studies* to the teaching of cultural studies (2008: 9 (3)).

DOES CULTURAL STUDIES HAVE A FUTURE?

6

I am not nostalgic for some previous moment of cultural studies; I do not read the history of cultural studies as a narrative of either progress or decline. I want to suggest that there have been moments when, for many different reasons and as a result of many different determinations, political intellectuals were able to more fully realize the project of cultural studies, without necessarily doing it self-consciously; in general, the history of cultural studies has been a history of mixed results. I presume that this is as it must be, and will always be the case. But it seems to me that in the contemporary moment, we might become more self-conscious of the project, and to take it up again. It is not a matter of berating cultural studies or those who claim to practice it, but of challenging us to think beyond the institutional constraints and habits to which we have become accustomed. (Lawrence Grossberg, *Cultural Studies in the Future Tense*, 2010: 66–7)

The title of this chapter poses a genuine question, in my view. There are plenty of folk, even inside the cultural studies project, who would suggest that cultural studies' future has now passed. To cite just two anecdotal examples from my own experience: it is at least a decade since I heard a relatively senior cultural studies personage seriously suggest that cultural studies was 'over', arguing that it had done its job of opening up the humanities and social sciences to new ways of thinking about culture, to recognizing the importance of understanding popular culture, and establishing a clearly critical account of the operation of the media. Unless cultural studies wanted to claim a disciplinary role for itself, the argument went, there was now nothing left for cultural studies to do. While that is not how I saw it, and still do not, I was struck (staggered, actually) by the cool rationality of that assessment. The second example: it is less than a year since a colleague of mine who works in American studies in the USA, doing what I would describe as a blend of cultural history and cultural studies, told me that she didn't know *anybody* in her sector of the profession who explicitly identified their work as cultural studies. Both of these comments shocked me at the time, indeed I still find the more recent one hard to believe, but it would be foolish not to recognize their implications: that a future for cultural studies, even in the short term, is far from assured.

Notwithstanding all of that, my personal answer to the question in my chapter title is 'Yes'. But that is only the starting point. The follow-up question – exactly what *kinds* of futures lie ahead for cultural studies – is more difficult to answer; for one thing, whatever future we might imagine must involve some changes to what cultural studies has become. That said, it seems to me, certainly in the short term and depending on the location, that cultural studies could survive, and perhaps even prosper, in three slightly different but not necessarily mutually exclusive modes:

- as a conventional, free-standing, discipline or interdiscipline engaged in delivering clearly defined programmes of teaching and research;
- as a broadly defined but institutionally contingent set of theoretical and methodological approaches used to deal with the problematic of 'culture' across disciplines and research fields;
- as the teaching and research 'project' of cultural studies with all the history, politics and self-consciousness that this implies.

Long term, I think, cultural studies will need to have all of these modes in operation if it is going to have a future. Let me explain why I take that view.

As I argued in Chapter 2, if cultural studies is to survive as a free-standing discipline or inter-discipline engaged in defined programmes of teaching and research, then establishing and maintaining its institutional base is fundamentally important. This has lately started to look a little more difficult than previously, as a result of the downturn in the university system in the USA due to the global financial crisis, and of new policy environments such as that created by the UK government's massive budget cuts to higher education. In the last year or two, we have seen at least one important programme of cultural studies in the USA closed down completely; this, in a context where cultural studies' institutional presence was minimal in the first place. In the UK, fields such as ours will be extremely vulnerable unless they can attract high levels of demand from fee-paying (and preferably international) students. Maintaining a free-standing, discrete disciplinary presence in such heavily commercialized environments is going to be a challenge, especially at the level of the undergraduate teaching programme.

On the other hand, cultural studies theory and research is probably very well placed to survive, in the short term at least, as a theoretical and methodological resource for other disciplines, areas or interdisciplinary fields. I suggested in the previous chapter that this has become a legitimate, if nonetheless secondary, role for cultural studies to play. As demonstrated in Chapter 1, it constitutes one of the avenues through which cultural studies has influenced the nature of theory and practice in a number of areas in the humanities and social sciences. It has, then, been valuable for the disciplines and research fields concerned and for extending the purchase of cultural studies itself (later in this chapter, I want to discuss this a little more). But it is a highly contingent role for cultural studies to play and its primary function is to work in the interests of the 'user' disciplines and research fields. In the long term, that mode of survival – if it turns out to be the only mode available – will inevitably lead to cultural studies' submersion within these disciplines and thus to the eventual disappearance of an independent identity for something called cultural studies. So, while this particular future does look quite easy to achieve, it could result in the end of cultural studies as a defined way of producing knowledge.

As for 'the project' of cultural studies, I should explain why I am using that phrase here as a device for distinguishing it from 'cultural studies' in general. In this context, I am using it as a means of pointing to the complications emerging from what I see as one of the more fundamental principles underpinning the beginnings of British cultural studies – indeed, what made its development so distinctive and valuable. While the Birmingham Centre for Contemporary Cultural Studies formation of cultural studies in the 1970s and 1980s had many distinguishing characteristics – the connection with left activism, the assertion of independence from the disciplines and from the institution, and, of course, the groundbreaking focus on the construction of everyday life – the one that I connect most with 'the project' of cultural studies is its claim to employ a mode of academic practice that is fundamentally committed to the social and political usefulness of the knowledge it produces. That is, the objectives of the cultural studies project are not only academic, but are also aimed at generating a public good as an outcome of its analysis.

Now, although this aspect of the practice of cultural studies is commonly invoked by just about everyone who identifies as cultural studies, the realities behind the rhetoric have – necessarily, perhaps inevitably – changed greatly over time. As cultural studies has grown, developed and mutated into diverse institutional and intellectual formations, the claim of broad political engagement has lost some of its plausibility. We may not want to admit it, but the insistence that cultural studies is political has, from time to time and in some contexts, worked more like a legitimating discourse than a description of what actually is the case. It is probably time we considered the proposition that, as cultural studies has found its place within the university, and as its activities have been more and more contained within the world of the university, the claim to be engaged in a wider cultural politics is just not as convincing as it might once have been. The 1990s' obsession with positionality, and perhaps the concurrent development of an unwarranted confidence in the broader political effectivity of academic discourses, produced versions of cultural studies that certainly nominated themselves as political but would be more accurately described as a genre of academic performance. My concern about what has become of the project of cultural studies, then, is to do with the gradual accretion of a cultural studies mythology that has effectively masked the realities of what has become of its practice.

Too often, this mythology is put to work generating discourses that are merely self-serving. This is the stuff that has drawn steady fire from our critics in other disciplines and, while we are understandably reluctant to echo these criticisms in our own internal debates, I think we have to admit that sometimes they are justified. As an example, let's consider what is perceived as cultural studies' notorious (and, obviously, irritating) confidence in its authority to talk on just about *anything* to do with culture – without necessarily having a strong research base on the particular topic. To some extent, I acknowledge, this does come with the territory: as a new field attempts to establish the distinctiveness of its mode of analysis and, in our case, the broad purchase of our conceptualization of culture. In the early days, such self-confidence could still seem admirable – naïve, perhaps, but enthusiastic and committed. Over time, and as the representatives of cultural studies have become more securely embedded in the university establishment, this kind of thing has begun to sound careerist rather than naïve, complacent rather than enthusiastic, and insouciant rather than committed, producing a form of preachy arrogance we would do well to leave behind us. Admittedly, as the practice of cultural studies moves more steadily towards defining its activities around research, such activity is less characteristic of the field, but we need to acknowledge that such a potential, and such practices, do exist and affect the purchase and credibility of our work.

Among the attractions of Larry Grossberg's recent book, *Cultural Studies in the Future Tense* (2010) is how unsentimental it is about acknowledging the limits to the likely sustainability of the cultural studies project. One of the dangers he warns against is the exaggerated sense of vocation that can drive cultural studies practitioners to claim more for their expertise than is legitimate or indeed plausible, and then to hector others into accepting such claims:

> I want to take an unpopular – but also incomplete – position, one that many of my friends and allies in cultural studies may not share: that it is not our job as analysts of the contemporary to offer a normative politics or even morally based political judgments, although it is sometimes unavoidable and perhaps necessary. But it is not my job – as a critical scholar – to tell people what they should be or desire. (Grossberg, 2010: 97)

Or, as he put it, more bluntly and arrestingly, in a comment during the question period at a conference session I attended recently: 'We are not priests! We don't get to tell people how to live their lives!' All of that said, what I am describing as the project of cultural studies is so fundamental to cultural studies' future that we must continually return to it, finding ways to refresh and invigorate it so that it can exercise a more productive influence over the practice of cultural studies. That is not a heritage preservation project, though – rather, it is a means of not losing sight of what matters.

Grossberg warns us that the cultural studies project does not have to be, should not be, an inherently conservative formation. Cultural studies is meant to be dynamic, mobile and useful; so, Grossberg argues that we must allow it to respond to the particular environments in which it operates:

> I am arguing that cultural studies takes its shape in response to its context – that cultural studies is a response in part to 'experienced' changes, to changing political challenges and demands,

as well as to emerging theoretical resources and debates. Without such a sense of the complexity of the project and history of cultural studies, one is likely to fall into a trap common to many of its critics ... of identifying all of cultural studies with a single vision ... (48)

This is very much the message of Chapter 5 in this book, my account of the process of cultural studies' internationalization. In terms of the institutional strategies it adopts for survival, cultural studies should explore every opportunity available to secure that survival. But, in order to succeed, those of us who work in cultural studies must also think more dispassionately about what cultural studies has become, how that is currently shaping its possible futures, and what might be done to ensure that it retains the capacity to actively choose and define those futures. In the following two sections of this chapter, I return to a central imperative for the practice of cultural studies that is in danger of being discarded in response to these adaptations and variations; then, I report upon a particular example of cultural studies in action which functioned as an enabling interdisciplinary language in order, paradoxically, to argue for the importance of cultural studies' investing in its disciplinary identity.

CULTURAL STUDIES AND THE PUBLIC GOOD

There are some contextually driven changes to the practices of cultural studies we do well to resist. Let us return to the criticism that Jim McGuigan made of what *he* believes has become of cultural studies: that it has lost its original commitment to 'critique in the public interest' (2006: 138). Such a way of thinking about the purpose of a humanities discipline is clearly on the decline now, particularly where McGuigan comes from. The UK is in the middle of a massive restructuring of the very idea of a university education at the moment. The implementation of the Browne report (2010) takes what had hitherto been a contested point of view (that an education in the humanities is a luxury, a private indulgence) to its logical but disturbing conclusion – disturbing, partly, because it seems so little contested by any beyond those directly affected. This situation is not confined to the UK, however. Although what I want to say in this section responds to changes in the rationales for higher education in both the UK and Australia, there are elements of these changes that will found in most places where cultural studies is taught. There is, then, a general tendency to be described even though it may vary in its details and in the extent of its applicability.

The deteriorating position of the liberal arts and humanities disciplines – that is, their losing battle against instrumentalist rationales for higher education and their steady decline in public and political support – has gone in tandem with the changes we have seen in the idea of the university over the last few decades. Crudely put, once, in an earlier period few of us can now remember, the university was regarded as itself constituting a public good: it developed the potential of the nation through the civilizing and modernizing process of the generation, dissemination, and transmission of knowledge. The humanities were located at the core of that process. They were at the beginning of the history of education as a civilizing activity, they were the custodians of national cultural traditions and heritage, their commitment to a universalist conception of the world disconnected them from vested interests, and their lack of commercial value, far from being a problem, was taken as a clear sign of their intellectual purity. Of course, we must not be too nostalgic about this; this is the conception of the humanities that produced the traditions cultural studies was established, in part, to oppose, and that went hand in hand with a regime of access to the university that was unashamedly elitist, gendered, classed and in some cases even racialized. So, it was worth contesting. However, the attempt to turn this around has coincided with a fundamental shift in the idea of the university. Rendering the university open to a larger, meritocratically selected, proportion of the population (on the face of it, a straightforwardly progressive idea), seems to have come at the cost of the slow embrace of a crudely vocationalist instrumentalism. This instrumentalism has participated in the production of a version of the university in which the primary purpose of the acquisition of an education is to equip the individual for employment. Initially, even within this version of the university, the humanities were still regarded as an appropriate and at times even a welcome inclusion despite the overwhelmingly utilitarian rationale. When times got tough, however, (and that, in the West, is where we are now) the incremental application of market criteria to the humanities disciplines was enough to gradually wear that welcome out.

At the same time as the idea of the university was mutating, the humanities disciplines were themselves changing. This happened in at least two directions: one was inclined towards a lively interdisciplinarity, and the other was aimed at fitting into the instrumentalist agenda. On the one hand, we had the developments in cultural and critical theory, which worked away at undermining the power of academic disciplines by nominating their theoretical bases and developing new forms of interdisciplinarity. This has been transformative and the modernization of the disciplines produced by the rise of cultural and critical theory is one of the most exciting intellectual developments of the post-war period. On the other hand, however, we had teaching programmes and research initiatives responding to the commercialization of the university by putting themselves well and truly on the market, prioritizing and exaggerating the applied and 'useful' elements of our fields, and gradually (if often only implicitly) disavowing anything which might be seen as distinctive (or indeed demanding) about the character and purpose of the liberal arts and humanities disciplines. Interestingly, and as noted earlier in this book, these two agendas sometimes coincided as universities restructured – using interdisciplinarity as a means of achieving administrative rationalization, cutting departments by merging them into multidisciplinary schools and so on.

What got lost in all of this is what is distinctive about these disciplinary fields – what I argued in Chapter 4 is in danger of being buried if cultural studies mutates into creative industries: the idea that there is an intellectual, ethical–moral purpose behind the production and distribution of knowledge that is directed towards the social and cultural wellbeing of a society, and not just its economic development. It is the kind of thinking that allowed the original (but, perhaps, not today's) audience of *Citizen Kane* to understand exactly what is meant when one of its characters tells Orson Welles' troubled tycoon, 'There's no trick to making money, if that's all you want to do.' Little wonder that an education system aimed with increasing singlemindedness at equipping its graduates with the capacity to make money should find that the knowledges it requires to do that are becoming more and more straightforward. Complexity, having something else 'you want to do', only gets in the way.

Cultural studies has been infected by this. On the one hand and on balance, it has probably been a positive thing that cultural studies has found it easier than most to align itself with the marketizing agenda, due to its genuine intellectual engagement with commercial culture, its legitimate association with the training of graduates for the media industries, and its principled contemporariness of focus. For much of what goes on under the name of cultural studies, this does not necessarily involve enormous conflicts of interest; indeed, it is probably an acceptable trade-off with the 'professional' subjects that has allowed us to do what we want while still delivering what the new university has required. On the other hand, at times this alignment may be too close for comfort. Jim McGuigan is not the only one to have noticed the 'discernible homology between the active subject of Cultural Studies and the sovereign consumer of free-market capitalism' (2006: 149). It would be naïve not to recognize that the forces which work on such an alignment can push us away, all too easily, from remembering that our work is fundamentally critical and that its purpose is to provide, first, a public good. We can see this in some of our teaching programmes. As I noted in Chapter 3, the loss of the excitement about cultural studies as an undergraduate programme may have many causes but among them has to be the difficulty of welding a critical discipline onto an industry training platform. Where the development of earning power rather than analytic power is the objective of the teaching programme, cultural studies risks simply becoming just another vocational option; gone is the ideal of teaching a politically engaged intellectual practice.

Cultural studies' relative success in an environment that is in general not hospitable to the humanities may have encouraged some of its practitioners to regard themselves as more or less immune from the forces that have hit the traditional disciplines, such as classics or foreign languages, with particular force. So, perhaps it seems that we can flirt with the market without having to give up much as a result. I don't think you can flirt with commercialization without being transformed by it. The sciences have known this for years, and are far more experienced at dealing with the resulting ambiguities – hence the complex procedures for ethical clearance and intellectual property rights, on the one hand, and the inevitable scandals about tainted research when they fail, on the other. We have limited experience of this, and few institutional systems to protect us, so we would do well to learn from other disciplines about how we handle the problem of commercial or government influence over our academic practice. There are issues of probity, academic independence, and moral rights here, but more importantly for us there is little point in the work we do simply supplementing government and industry's 'already well-established administrative and instrumental agendas for research' (McGuigan, 2006: 142).

More worryingly, I don't think that we can rely on a deep well of community support for cultural studies – no matter how cool and contemporary it might seem to us or to some of our students. Watching debates about the public attitude to the humanities now over many years, I have formed the view that the most of the community who might support the humanities in principle still thinks that the humanities are the traditional disciplines – literary studies, history and so on. They might well, eventually and if pushed, be inclined to fight for the survival of these disciplines; I don't think they would fight for cultural studies. I suspect that the version of cultural studies that is routinely represented in the popular press (an obscure, elitist, form of criticism usually labelled as 'postmodern') is the one that sticks. This is particularly the case in the UK where the attitude taken to media and cultural studies by the print media in particular is actively and unremittingly antagonistic. This is not a safe position to be in and so if anyone in cultural studies thinks they can stand back and watch their old enemies (elite, traditional disciplines such as English) being put to the sword by neoliberal higher education policies without worrying too much about this happening to themselves, they are wrong. Hence, my concern about the potential for the unintended consequences of Chapter 4 to put a stake through the heart of the whole cultural studies enterprise, because it is so complicit with the direction of neoliberal education policy, because it is so shortsightedly disinterested in the public benefit of a critical education for its own sake, and because it sees economic development as the primary public purpose that education can serve. The public good that cultural studies should achieve does not have a place in that enterprise; it should occupy pride of place in ours.

AN INTERDISCIPLINARY *LINGUA FRANCA*

In Chapter 5, I referred to the role that cultural studies had taken, in some contexts, of contributing to other fields by providing an interdisciplinary means of dealing with the general problematic of culture. The example I used there was that of Latin American studies, but we also saw in Chapter 1 that this was also essentially the role it played in American studies in the

1980s and 1990s. It provided an already elaborated set of theoretical protocols, a sophisticated set of debates about understanding culture, and a number of established methodological strategies – this last attribute notwithstanding all the talk of cultural studies being a method-free zone. While I earlier referred to this as a secondary role for cultural studies and expressed the view that it would be dangerous if it were to be the *only* role that cultural studies was to play, I think there is every reason to see it, nonetheless, as an important and legitimate role. Let me briefly outline a project with which I have been involved that may help to demonstrate why.

In 2004, the Australian Research Council set up a programme to fund research networks. Initially, this was conceived as a strategy for sharing the use of large infrastructure, expensive equipment, large datasets and so on as a means of maximizing the utility of what had been substantial government investments. In order to include the humanities and social sciences, however, the research network programme also had to include people; it did this, rather sweetly, by including as one of its objectives 'bringing people together'. This meant that it would fund travel and other costs required for researchers around Australia to meet to share ideas and develop collaborative projects. It did not actually fund research, but it facilitated the planning of projects for which funding might be sought. Given the lack of a collaborative research culture in the humanities generally, it was always going to be hard to find a viable and convincing intellectual formation likely to secure funding from this programme. Cultural studies, at the time, was one of the most vibrant and one of the more successful competitors for research funding among the humanities research fields in Australia, and so it seemed worth applying for a research network that was organized around it. The problem lay in finding a collaborative programme that could be convincingly led by cultural studies.

I was the convenor of this application. It was built on the premise that cultural studies would provide the theoretical and conceptual tools to enable a range of disciplines in the humanities and social sciences that shared a central interest in understanding culture – cultural studies, cultural anthropology, cultural geography, cultural history – to work together in new and valuable ways. The application was successful and the Cultural Research Network (CRN) was established in 2005, with funding until the end of 2009. It comprised 43 researchers from these fields, at the outset, and grew to a total of 75 over the funding period. Few, if any, of these researchers, had ever taken part in a collaborative project; certainly few would have collaborated with anyone from another discipline. Those who didn't come from cultural studies – which were the majority – collectively carried the full repertoire of all the usual suspicions, jealousies and misunderstandings of cultural studies. The task (or at least the one that is most relevant to this discussion) was to teach each discipline what the others might offer. The notion of 'cultural research' provided the common element which made such a conversation possible. There was no common method or approach, however. What was required was a means of communicating between disciplines that would enable that common approach to be developed – contingently, in relation to the demands of the specific project. The great benefit of cultural studies in this context is what might be described as its relatively promiscuous disciplinary habit; it has been omnivorous (to move to a safer metaphor) in its relations with other disciplines and so it was unfazed at this kind of lateral intellectual movement. Furthermore, the widespread currency across the contemporary humanities of the theoretical and philosophical concepts that had been so central to the development of cultural studies meant that there was already a relatively familiar body of concepts shared between all of these fields. They might have differed on how to define or use these concepts but not on their importance. Finally, the combination of the operation of the assumptions behind the cultural studies project, and the careful selection of the participants from the other disciplines, meant that there was an unspoken objective behind all the research discussed – that it had the public interest at its heart. Cultural studies enabled the conversation between disciplines: it became the theoretical or disciplinary *lingua franca* that allowed them to talk about how they wanted to understand and approach that common objective[1].

The details of how that happened are probably relatively unimportant for what I want to say about this here. But, largely, it simply involved exposing people to the interests of their colleagues in other disciplines, and to their modes of dealing with the task of prosecuting those interests. The very first network meeting had speakers from each of the discipline groups explaining what it meant 'to know' in their discipline: this highlighted the common territory, opened up disciplinary assumptions for interrogation from outside, and also demonstrated that some disciplines seemed to 'know' things that others didn't, and in ways that others hadn't come across before. Of course, there was some jostling for position, and some turning up of noses when one discipline heard what they considered to be a sign of the lack of sophistication of another. But this did not last – largely because of the care with which what was actually a kind of academic speed-dating was managed: the complementary matching of interest and expertise across disciplinary divides, and the arrangements which rendered this matching operable. The initial process was simple: large workshop meetings with topic areas opened up for conversation, and entry to that conversation offered to all participants. Over time, project groups were created, projects happened, and research funding followed. Over the five-year period of funding, 57 members of this group of researchers won national research grants; virtually all of these were collaborative, involving multidisciplinary teams achieving things collectively they could never have achieved by themselves. Without cultural studies providing them with a language for talking about their work, this would not have happened[2].

This proved to an extremely worthwhile venture and it has helped build a particular kind of future for cultural research in Australia – a future in which cross-disciplinary collaboration on topics in the public interest has become the norm. The qualities of cultural studies – possibly, in fact, the particular qualities of Australian cultural studies (such as its relative comfort with empirical research methods) – proved to be peculiarly useful in this project and the whole humanities and social sciences sector has benefited as a result.

Nonetheless, it is also important to reiterate the point I made earlier on; which is that while this is something cultural studies can do now, and should do now, this is not *all* it should do now. Of itself, it is not going to be enough to ensure cultural studies' survival; and of itself, perhaps, it may not even be enough to support a vigorous case for its survival. While this kind of activity certainly generates new possibilities both from within and outside cultural studies, it also has to be acknowledged that the eventual effect will be for cultural studies to be submerged within those disciplines that have a stronger institutional presence, a more structured approach to training their postgraduates and younger researchers, and a more clearly defined identity for undergraduates. There are many disciplines that are stronger in all these aspects than cultural studies. From where I stand, this is a worrying situation. The cross-disciplinary benefits to be offered by cultural studies now are substantial but, paradoxically, the potential to keep delivering those benefits depends upon cultural studies maintaining a substantially independent teaching and research identity, and its own theoretical and developmental agenda.

What cultural studies brought to cultural research was a focus on the construction of everyday life that was driven by specific sets of theoretical concerns which took us into new domains of the practices of everyday life – most obviously, but not only, popular culture and the media. As cultural studies works with other disciplines on the shared problematic of culture, the benefits of that focus are considerable; as we have seen in many locations in this book, the work that cultural studies has done for its own purposes has been frequently and usefully appropriated by many other disciplines for their own purposes. For this to continue, though, cultural studies has to maintain itself, effectively, as a discipline: this will enable it to continue to generate the insights deemed necessary to the project of cultural studies which, almost by definition, are not going to be deemed necessary in the first instance by other disciplines. In terms of thinking through the long-term prospects for the future, this needs to be seriously considered.

CONCLUSION

The best guide to the future of cultural studies, of course, lies in the present. As a field, we have not talked very much about what we do in the present as an everyday professional practice. Instead, we have focused on the theories and approaches which interest us, and which in most cases have drawn us to cultural studies as a means of understanding the social and textual practices of others. What I have wanted to address in this book is slightly different territory: where the practice of cultural studies is about designing teaching programmes, teaching and training our students, arguing for cultural studies within faculty or school committees, developing research projects and applying for grants, writing abstracts for conferences or submitting book outlines to prospective publishers – that is, undertaking a professional life as an academic in cultural studies. To some extent, the residual romanticism that still lingers around the project of cultural studies overlooks and perhaps undervalues these kinds of everyday realities. It is highly ironic that this should be the case, of course, given cultural studies' role in rescuing the everyday as a subject for academic analysis.

Cultural studies is among the humanities disciplines where academics' everyday practice has become increasingly professionalized, strategic and institutionally oriented – this is particularly so for younger people, entering a workplace in which these attributes have become ever more important to one's continuing employment. That has its drawbacks: new academics are often given unrealistic targets for their output and their impact; they are required to become well published almost immediately upon completing the apprenticeship of the PhD; and the oppression of the performance indicator or the unpredictability of the tenure process requires them to continually monitor their progress in ways their predecessors rarely had to do, let alone at such an early stage in their careers. This cohort of teachers and researchers are acutely aware that they do not have the option of disregarding the institutional indicators used by their university to calibrate their careers. Senior academics in the field have a duty of care to these young people to provide advice and mentoring so that they might successfully manage their relation to their institution. In general, there is not a lot of evidence that this duty has either been accepted or discharged. Largely, the young researcher is left to deal with their anxieties alone. An area where this is evident is in the management of the track record of research publications. The publications profile has been of particular importance to cultural studies scholars. The expansion of publishers' cultural studies lists has been dramatic; it may have peaked in terms of the numbers of books published during the 1990s, but it has greatly diversified in its subject matter and in its internationalization since then. Consequently, in some markets, it has been easier to get published in cultural studies than in many other disciplines (literary studies, for instance), and so it has become a routine expectation of recent PhD graduates in cultural studies that they get that first book contract as soon as possible. This, while learning how to teach, applying for research grants, presenting at conferences and providing service to the profession. In this respect, cultural studies is at the leading edge of both the good and the bad sides of the contemporary university – it is one of the areas where early career researchers have been making an exceptionally powerful contribution, but it is also at the centre of the escalation of the demands of the workplace and their infiltration into our private lives that has affected more than just those working in the academy[3].

I could go on at greater length here, further unpacking the complications we can see in what cultural studies has become. But, as I conclude this book, I want to return to review some of its core arguments, the issues I have been highlighting as those which should concern us in cultural studies. In Chapter 1, I tried to give some sense of what we might count among the achievements of cultural studies so far, as a prelude to the book's primary task of outlining a critique of the practices of cultural studies in the university today. The two main areas upon which I focused – cultural studies' development of ways of analysing the media and popular culture, and cultural studies development of transposable approaches and methods that have been taken up as a means of dealing with the idea of culture in a range of interdisciplinary fields – are both, it seems to me, incontestably ones where cultural studies has had an impact. However, the point I make at the end, using the quotation from Stuart Hall where he bemoans the number of cultural studies scholars writing analyses of *The Sopranos*, directs us towards significant problems in the contemporary practice of cultural studies. As I see it, the Hall criticism has two dimensions. The first implicitly questions the choice of topic (*The Sopranos*) for the contemporary practice of cultural studies: perhaps, from Hall's point of view, the intensity of the attention given to this popular television series is unwarranted because it is too trivial, too influenced by fan–critic fashion, or simply too driven by personal enthusiasms. Whichever of these applies, it is clear that Hall is suggesting that the level of interest is disproportionate to the claims that have been made for the series' significance. The second dimension is the more important, it seems to me. This, I take it, accuses cultural studies of mistaking an analytic method for a political purpose; that is, textual analyses of prominent television programmes are being offered as ends in themselves, rather than as modes of accessing deeper structural, cultural and political tendencies. Once again, this suggests cultural studies is becoming a performative or perhaps even an aesthetic, rather than a political, practice. I should insist here that I am far from arguing that there is no place at all for such work;

rather, I see it as crossing the unspoken boundaries between the interests of cultural studies and those that are legitimately and profitably prosecuted through television studies, screen studies or film studies. In the end, in my view and perhaps not everyone would agree with this, freestanding and evaluative textual analysis is no longer a primary activity for cultural studies[4].

Chapter 2 began the task of examining what's become of the practice of cultural studies today by focusing on its ambivalent relation to disciplinarity, one of the continuing themes of *What's Become of Cultural Studies?*. As I have stated on a number of occasions in this book, cultural studies has a history of taking a principled line on disciplinarity – resisting it as a constraint upon free intellectual enquiry and as a repressive form of institutionalization. The practice, however, has been less principled, as cultural studies has, *de facto*, acquired many of the characteristics of a discipline. There are good reasons for this. In terms of our actual engagement with the institutions in which we work, we can see that the establishment of disciplinary status has useful knock-on effects that we might want to think about before we reject them out of hand. Disciplines help us to access research grants, and provide the structure for state-run quality assessment processes; the institutional trappings of a discipline are more or less mandatory for the establishment of discrete teaching programmes, schools or departments, defined teaching and research positions, career paths and the like. The refusal of disciplinary status, on the other hand, makes access to every one of these things more difficult. More worryingly, though, the chapter focuses on the impact that the resistance to disciplinarity has upon our capacity to properly train our postgraduate students, to orient them within the broad intellectual coordinates of the field, and thus to equip them for teaching and research positions in the university. The limits to interdisciplinarity as a means of training the next generation of teachers, and, indeed, the limits to interdisciplinarity as an epistemological strategy, are revealed in some of the ways many cultural studies graduate programmes have been designed and taught.

Ultimately, I argued, cultural studies, like some other interdisciplinary initiatives that have developed since the 1960s in the humanities and social sciences, will have to negotiate the contradiction between a cultural studies that wants to remain free of the ties of disciplinarity and the institutional reality that requires it to embrace at least some of the protocols of a discipline in order to function as a viable organizational entity.

Chapter 3 took as its text a fictional but (I suggest) typical introductory course in cultural studies, Cultural Studies 101, as a means of highlighting problems in the contemporary teaching of cultural studies to undergraduates. The reproduction of a canon of cultural studies' theoretical texts, the teaching of cultural studies theory as a body of writing rather than a set of concepts, and a form of elitism shaping the student–teacher relation, all run against the grain of the idea of cultural studies but they are all evident in a large number of cultural studies teaching programmes around the world. The privileging of critique is also widely evident; in some instances it becomes the primary skill for cultural studies students to master. It is also an area of student performance where we tend to be highly prescriptive about what we expect from them. We need to renew our commitment to more open and productive models of pedagogic practice that enable students to capitalize on their own experience of the cultures of everyday life. Cultural Studies 101 reminds me, chillingly, of the pedagogic and disciplinary structures which were used to mystify and sustain the teaching of English Literature 101 40 years ago. Cultural studies teaching needs to do more to draw upon its students' own capacities, while demonstrating cultural studies' potential to create new understandings of aspects of experience our students may well have taken for granted. This is going to take a much more serious commitment to an engaged, lively, student-centred pedagogy than we now commonly encounter. It is not unusual for cultural studies teaching to simply consist of setting a canonical reading and providing an occasion for its exegesis. We can do better than that, and we need to, if we want our students to recognize both the productiveness and the availability of cultural studies' fundamental conceptual apparatus. Finally, in this chapter, I referred to the downgrading of teaching within cultural studies scholars' conceptualization of their professional role; there is a possibility that the contemporary privileging of research as the most important of our activities has played a part in generating a complacent attitude to the quality of the teaching we provide to our undergraduate students in cultural studies.

Among the reasons why this might matter – and there are many – is the pragmatic observation that we need to be teaching at least as well as our competition. In Chapter 4, I argued that some of this competition has come from within cultural studies itself but is now mutating in ways that runs directly contrary to the politics of the project of cultural studies – specifically, its commitment to critique in the public interest. There are two dimensions to this chapter's argument. The first contests the claims made by those working in the areas identified with convergence culture, new media studies and creative industries to be the next developmental stage for the broad fields of cultural and media studies. All these approaches nominate the present conjuncture as the occasion of a paradigm shift that has dramatically rearranged the power differentials which structure our relation to the media, and attribute to new media technologies the capacity to generate substantial social and political change. This latter claim is more extensively contested elsewhere, and in its own terms (Turner, 2010), so I don't focus on that aspect in this chapter. Rather, the first point of focus in Chapter 4 is upon the legitimacy of the claim to be the next stage of development for cultural studies. That claim is refuted, and the economistic focus of the goals of creative industries, in particular, are accused of surrendering the core political objective of cultural studies.

The second dimension concerns the quality and provenance of the teaching programmes mounted in support of these paradigms. The academic flimsiness of the creative industries and new media programmes I examined for this chapter proved to be quite shocking, in fact. I had not realized how little ground there was for the claiming of a cultural studies heritage, until I began searching the undergraduate programmes for evidence of that heritage. I found very little; indeed, in some cases, I found very little to suggest that these programmes bore allegiance to *any* academic tradition. Where my critique of the cultural studies programmes for undergraduates pointed to their lack of interest in their students, and to the unrealistically high expectations of students' ability to negotiate demanding theoretical texts, the problem for the creative industries and new media programmes was the reverse: that is, they were so excessively focused on vocational training for their students that in some instances there was little room for academic content. Nonetheless, it is evident that there is a growing market for these courses, and while it may well be a relatively short-lived market, there is also evidence to suggest that students who might once have chosen cultural studies are being attracted to these programmes. Given how poorly they fill the intellectual space occupied by cultural studies, and given the indications that they will fill that space at the expense of cultural studies, this is a trend which should be of great concern.

A more positive story was told in Chapter 5, however. There is a long history of debate about the internationalization of cultural studies, which focuses around the danger of losing cultural studies' located politics on the one hand, and the universalism implied by thinking of the process as a 'translation' of (British, or Anglo–American) cultural studies into new national, regional or geo-linguistic contexts, on the other hand. It is true that the dominant Western versions of cultural studies do need to be reminded that important and distinctive work goes on elsewhere, and has done for decades. As a contribution towards that end, this chapter provides a brief account of the Inter-Asia Cultural Studies movement as an example of an 'indigenized' form of cultural studies that has been shaped in important ways by the specific context of its own national and regional locations. Far from being merely a translation of the hegemonic version of cultural studies into a local or regional dialect, the Inter-Asia Cultural Studies movement demonstrates the adaptability and mobility of cultural studies modes of producing knowledge while providing the international field of cultural studies with new models of research and political practice. The debates over internationalization are not resolved by this example, of course; in fact, it suggests that these contradictions may well be constitutive of the contemporary practice of cultural studies – something that does not discount the likelihood of these contradictions also being highly productive. The Inter-Asia example is not offered as a model for others necessarily to follow, but it may take us a little further towards accepting a greater diversity in our view of what cultural studies can become; perhaps, even towards embracing the possibility of a much more transnational and comparative practice of cultural studies in the future.

The account I have presented in this book is one that, I hope, properly acknowledges what cultural studies has so far achieved even though it focuses on the challenges it faces in the future. Since the latter is my primary concern, the dominant register of the account is critical. The intention behind the criticism is to assist in the renovation of that customized and souped-up vehicle of cultural studies we encountered in Chapter 1, and help it serve fully its original purposes, the pressing needs of the present and those of the future. As a long-time friend of cultural studies, I hope that these ideas will then be taken in the spirit in which they are offered: as a means of opening up debate about the possible character and carriage of a future for cultural studies.

NOTES

1 The CRN had a number of objectives and this is only one. A further objective that is worth mentioning here, even if it is a little digressive, is the focus on developing early career researchers. A distinctive feature of the CRN was its goal of bringing together what was a highly successful generation of baby-boomer cultural studies practitioners with a cohort of younger researchers from around the country. With the 'stars' tending to be concentrated in a limited number of locations, many of the early career researchers in regional and minor campuses had little

access to the leaders in their fields. The CRN set out to change that and to a great extent succeeded.

2 Among the work that wouldn't have happened is a highly innovative collaboration among cultural historians, cultural geographers, cultural studies and cultural policy researchers on the cultures of rural communities in Australia. Some of this work is collected in a special issue of *Cultural Studies Review* edited by Clifton Evers, Andrew Gorman-Murray and Emily Potter on 'Rural Cultural Studies' (2010, 16: (1)); and in a special issue of *Australian Humanities Review* (2008, 45: November) again on 'Rural Cultural Studies', edited by David Carter, Kate Darian-Smith, and Andrew Gorman-Murray.

3 See Melissa Gregg's forthcoming study, *Work's Intimacy* (Polity, 2011).

4 I do think it was once. Textual analysis proved to be a crucial analytic methodology for cultural studies in its first decade or so, and its capacity to generate new kinds of information and interpretations was one of the exciting new potentials the field could offer. It has become more commonplace now, and the novelty of what it can tell us has gone.

REFERENCES

Ang, I. (1990) 'Culture and communication', *European Journal of Communication*, 5 (2/3): 239–61.

Ang, I. and Stratton, J. (1996a) 'Asianizing Australia: Notes towards a critical transnationalism in cultural studies', *Cultural Studies*, 10 (1): 16–36.

Ang, I. and Stratton, J. (1996b) 'A cultural studies without guarantees', *Cultural Studies*, 10 (1): 71–7.

Bennett, T. (1989) 'Culture: theory and policy', *Culture and Policy*, 1: 5–8.

Bennett, T. (1992) 'Putting policy into cultural studies', in L. Grossberg, C. Nelson and P. Treichler (eds), *Cultural Studies*. New York, NY: Routledge.

Bennett, T. (1998) 'Cultural studies: A reluctant discipline', *Cultural Studies*, 12 (4): 528–45.

Bennett, T. and Woollacott, J. (1987) *Bond and Beyond: The Political Career of a Popular Hero*. London: Methuen.

Bennett, T., Boyd-Bowman, S., Mercer, C. and Woollacott, J. (eds) (1981) *Popular Television and Film*. London: BFI/Open University Press.

Berger, J. (1972) *Ways of Seeing*. London: BBC/Penguin.

Bérubé, M. (1992) 'Pop goes the academy: Cult studs fights the power', *Village Voice Literary Supplement*, 104: 10–14.

Bérubé, M. (2009) 'What's the matter with cultural studies? The popular discipline loses its bearings', *The Chronicle Review, The Chronicle of Higher Education*, September 14. Available at: http://chronicle.com/article/Whats-the-Matter-With/48334/ (last accessed 25 September 2009).

Bourdieu, P. and Wacquant, L. (1999) 'The cunning of imperialist reason', *Theory, Culture and Society*, 16 (1): 45–8.

Brabazon, T. (2008) *Thinking Popular Culture: War, Terrorism and Writing*. London: Ashgate.

Browne, J. (2010) The Independent Review of Higher Education Funding and Student Finance, www.webarchive.nationalarchives.gov.uk/+/hereview.independent.gov.uk/hereview// (last accessed 9 May 2011).

Bruns, A. (2008) *Blogs, Wikipedia, Second Life and Beyond: From Production to Produsage*. New York: Peter Lang.

Budianta, M. (2010) 'Shifting the geographies of knowledge: the unfinished project of *Inter-Asia Cultural Studies*', *Inter-Asia Cultural Studies*, 11 (2): 174–7.

Campora, M. (2009) 'From the Art House to the Multiplex: An exploration of multiform cinema', unpublished PhD dissertation, University of Queensland.

Carey, J.W. (1989) *Communication as Culture: Essays on Media and Society*. Boston: Unwin Hyman.

Carter, D., Darian-Smith, K. and Gorman-Murray, A. (eds) (2008) 'Rural cultural studies', *Australian Humanities Review*, Special Issue, 45, November.

Chen, K.H. (1996a) 'Cultural studies and the politics of internationalization: an interview with Stuart Hall', in D. Morley and K.H. Chen (eds), *Stuart Hall: Critical Dialogues in Cultural Studies*. London: Routledge, pp. 392–410.

Chen, K.H. (1996b) 'The formations of a diasporic intellectual: an interview with Stuart Hall', in D. Morley and K.H. Chen (eds), *Stuart Hall: Critical Dialogues in Cultural Studies*. London: Routledge, pp. 484–503.

Chen, K.H. (1996c) 'Not yet the postcolonial era: The [super] nation-state and transnationalism of cultural studies: Response to Ang and Stratton', *Cultural Studies*, 10 (1): 37–70.

Chen, K.H. (1998) 'The decolonization question' in K.H. Chen (ed.), *Trajectories: Inter-Asia Cultural Studies*. London: Routledge, pp. 1–53.

Chen, K.H. (2010) 'Living with Tensions: Notes on the Inter-Asia movement', presented at 'Reflections and Imaginations': The 10th Anniversary Symposium of *Inter-Asia Cultural Studies: Movements*, April, Chiao Tung University, Hsinchu, Taiwan.

Chen, K.H. and Chua, B.H. (eds) (2007) *The Inter-Asia Cultural Studies Reader*. London: Routledge.

Ching, L. (2010) '*Inter-Asia Cultural Studies* and the decolonial turn', *Inter-Asia Cultural Studies*, 11 (2): 184–7.

Clarke, J. (1991) *New Times and old Enemies: Essays on Cultural Studies and America*. London: Routledge.

Clegg, S.C. (2001) 'The history of the book: An undisciplined discipline?' *Renaissance Quarterly*, 22 March.

Couldry, N. (2000) *Inside Culture: Re-imagining the Method of Cultural Studies*. London: Sage.

Cunningham, S. (1992) *Framing Culture: Criticism and Policy in Australia*. Sydney: Allen and Unwin.

Cunningham, S. (2002) 'From cultural to creative industries: Theory, industry and policy implications', *Media International Australia*, 102: 54–65.

Cunningham, S. (2004) 'The creative industries after cultural policy: A genealogy and some possible preferred futures', *International Journal of Cultural Studies*, 7 (1): 105–16.

Cunningham, S., Banks, J. and Potts, J. (2008) 'Cultural economy: the shape of the field', in H. Anheier and R. Isaar (eds), *The Cultural Economy*. London: Sage, pp. 15–26.

D'Arcy, C.C. (2009) '"A room of one's own"?: Cultural studies' relationship to institutionalization and disciplinarity in Spain', *Cultural Studies*, 23 (5–6): 855–72.

Department of Culture, Media and Sport (1998) *The Creative Industries Mapping Document*. London: Department of Culture, Media and Sport.

Du Gay, P., Hall, S., Janes, L., Mackay, H. and Negus, K. (1997) *Doing Cultural Studies: The Story of the Sony Walkman.* London: Sage.

Evers, C., Gorman-Murray, A. and Potter, E. (eds) (2010) 'Rural cultural studies', Special Issue of *Cultural Studies Review*, 16 (1) March.

Federal Communications Commission (2010) *Sixth Broadband Deployment Report,* June 20, Washington DC.

Ferguson, M. and Golding, P. (eds) (1997) *Cultural Studies in Question.* London: Sage.

Finnane, A. (2007) *Changing Clothes in China: Fashion, nation, history.* London: Hurst.

Finnane, A. and McLaren, A. (eds) (1999) *Dress, Sex and Text in Chinese Culture.* Melbourne: Monash Asia Institute.

Fiske, J. (1980) *Introduction to Communication.* London: Methuen.

Fiske, J. (1989) *Understanding Popular Culture.* Boston, MA: Unwin Hyman.

Fiske, J. and Hartley, J. (1978) *Reading Television.* London: Methuen.

Fiske, J., Hodge, B. and Turner, G. (1987) *Myths of Oz: Reading Australian Popular Culture.* Sydney: Allen and Unwin.

Flew, T., Hawkins, G. and Jacka, E. (eds) (1994) 'The policy moment', *Media Information Australia*, Special Issue, 73, August.

Florida, R. (2002) *The Rise of the Creative Class: And How it's Transforming Work, Leisure, Community and Everyday Life.* New York, NY: Basic Books.

Fornas, J. (2010) 'Continents of cultural studies – unite in diversity! Comparing Asian and European perspectives', *Inter-Asia Cultural Studies*, 11 (2): 214–20.

Frankovits, A. (1987) 'Letters', *Screen*, 28: 122–4.

Gauntlett, D. (2007) 'Media Studies 2.0', *Theory.org*, 24 February. Available at: www.theory.org.uk/mediastudies2-print.htm (last accessed 16 December 2008).

Gledhill, C. and Williams, W. (eds) (2000) *Reinventing Film Studies.* London: Arnold.

Gray, A. (2003) *Research Practice in Cultural Studies: Ethnographic Methods and Lived Cultures.* London: Sage.

Grossberg, L. (1997) *Dancing in Spite of Myself: Essays on Popular Culture.* Durham, NC: Duke University Press.

Grossberg, L. (2010) *Cultural Studies in the Future Tense.* Durham, NC: Duke University Press.

Grossberg, L., Nelson, C. and Treichler, P. (eds) (1992) *Cultural Studies.* New York, NY: Routledge.

Gunning, T. (1986) 'The cinema of attractions: Early films, the spectator and the avant-garde', *Wide Angle*, 8 (3–4): 630–70.

Hall, S. (1980) 'Recent developments in theories of language and ideology: a critical note' in S. Hall, D. Hobson, A. Lowe and P. Willis (eds), *Culture, Media, Language.* London: Hutchison, pp. 156–62.

Hall, S. (1992) 'Cultural studies and its theoretical legacies' in L. Grossberg, C. Nelson and P. Treichler (eds), *Cultural Studies*. New York, NY: Routledge, pp. 277–94.

Hartley, J. (2004) 'The "value chain of meaning" and the new economy', *International Journal of Cultural Studies*, 7 (1): 129–41.

Hartley, J. (2008) 'The future is an open future: Cultural studies at the end of the 'Long Twentieth Century' and the beginning of the 'Chinese Century', *Cultural Science*, 1 (1): 1–21.

Hartley, J. (2009a) (ed.) *Creative Industries*. Malden, MA: Blackwell.

Hartley, J. (2009b) *The Uses of Digital Literacy*. St Lucia: University of Queensland Press.

Hartley, J. and Pearson, R. (eds) (2000) *American Cultural Studies: A Reader*. Oxford: Oxford University Press.

Hartley, J. and Montgomery, L. (2009) 'Fashion as consumer entrepreneurship: Emergent risk culture, social network markets and the launch of *Vogue* in China', *Chinese Journal of Communication*, 2 (1): 61–76.

Hesmondhalgh, D. (2007) *Cultural Industries: An Introduction*, 2nd edn. London: Sage.

Hills, M. (2005) *How to do Things with Cultural Theory*. London: Hodder Arnold.

Hindman, M. (2009) *The Myth of Digital Democracy*. Princeton, NJ: Princeton University Press.

Inter-Asia Cultural Studies (2000) 'Editorial Statement', 1 (1): 5–6.

Jenkins, H. (1992) *Textual Poachers: Television Fans and Participatory Culture*. New York, NY: Routledge.

Jenkins, H. (2004) 'The cultural logic of media convergence', *International Journal of Cultural Studies*, 7 (1): 33–44.

Jenkins, H. (2006) *Convergence Culture: Where Old and New Media Collide*. New York, NY: New York University Press.

Johnson, R., Chambers, D., Raghuran, P. and Ticknell, E. (2004) *The Practice of Cultural Studies*. London: Sage.

Katz, E. and Scannell, P. (eds) (2009) 'The end of television? Its impact on the world (so far)', *Annals of the American Academy of Political and Social Science*, Special Issue, 625, September.

Keane, M. (2009) 'Creative industries in China: four perspectives on social transformation', *International Journal of Cultural Policy*, 15 (4): 431–43.

Kilgore, D.W.D. (1997) 'Undisciplined multiplicity: The relevance of an American cultural studies', *American Studies*, 38 (2): 31–40.

Klinger, B. (1994) *Melodrama and Meaning: History, Culture and the Films of Douglas Sirk*. Bloomington, IN: Indiana University Press.

Kuhn, A. (1984) 'Women's genres', *Screen*, 25 (1): 18–28.

Lamont, M. (2009) *How Professors Think: Inside the Curious World of Academic Judgment*. Cambridge, MA: Harvard University Press.

Lipsitz, G. (1990) 'Listening to learn and learning to listen: popular culture, cultural theory and American studies', *American Quarterly*, 42 (4): 615–36.

Lotz, A. (2007) *The Television Will Be Revolutionized*. New York, NY: New York University Press.

Louie, K. (2002) *Theorizing Chinese Masculinity: Society and Gender in China*. Cambridge: Cambridge University Press.

Mackie, V. (2003) *Feminism in Modern Japan: Citizenship, Embodiment and Sexuality*. Cambridge: Cambridge University Press.

Marginson, S. and Considine, M. (2000) *The Enterprise University: Power, Governance and Reinvention in Australia*. Cambridge: Cambridge University Press.

Martin, F. (2003) *Interpreting Everyday Culture*. London: Arnold.

McCabe, C. (2007) 'Interview with Stuart Hall', *Critical Quarterly*, 50 (1–2): 12–42.

McGuigan, J. (1992) *Cultural Populism*. London: Routledge.

McGuigan, J. (1997) *Cultural Methodologies*. London: Sage.

McGuigan, J. (2006) 'The politics of cultural studies and cool capitalism,' *Cultural Politics*, 2 (2): 137–58.

McRobbie, A. (1994) *Postmodernism and Popular Culture*. London: Routledge.

Miller, T. (2004) 'A view from a fossil: The new economy, creativity and consumption – two or three things I don't believe in', *International Journal of Cultural Studies*, 7 (1): 55–66.

Miller, T. (2009a) 'Approach with caution and proceed with care: campaigning for the US Presidency "after TV"', in G. Turner and J. Tay (eds), *Television Studies after TV: Understanding Television in the Post-broadcast Era*. London: Routledge, pp. 75–82.

Miller, T. (2009b) 'From creative to cultural industries', *Cultural Studies*, 23 (1): 88–99.

Morley, D. (1980) 'Texts, readers, subjects' in S. Hall, D. Hobson, A. Lowe and P. Willis (eds), *Culture, Media, Language*. London: Hutchison, pp. 163–73.

Morley, D. (1998) 'So-called cultural studies: Dead-ends and reinvented wheels', *Cultural Studies*, 12 (4): 476–97.

Morley. D. and Ang, I. (1989) 'Mayonnaise culture and other follies', *Cultural Studies*, 3 (2): 133–44.

Morris, M. (1990) 'Banality in Cultural Studies' in P. Mellencamp (ed.), *Logics of Television: Essays in Cultural Criticism*. London: BFI, pp. 14–43.

Morris, M. (2010) 'Inter-Asian banality and education', *Inter-Asia Cultural Studies*, 11 (2): 157–64.

Morris, M. and Wright, H. (2009) 'Introduction: Transnationalism and cultural studies', *Cultural Studies*, 23 (5–6): 689–93.

Nightingale, V. (1989) 'What's ethnographic about ethnographic cultural studies?', *Australian Journal of Communication*, 16: 50–63.

O'Connor, A. (1996) 'The problem of American cultural studies', in J. Storey (ed.), *What is Cultural Studies?: A Reader*. London: Arnold, pp. 187–97.

O'Connor, J. (2009) 'Creative industries: A new direction?', *International Journal of Cultural Policy*, 15 (4): 387–402.

O'Connor, J. (in press) 'Enlightenment, post-Fordism and post-materialist consumption: Creative industries in China', *Regional Studies*.

O'Connor, J. and Xin, G. (2006) 'A new modernity: the arrival of "creative industries" in China', *International Journal of Cultural Studies*, 9 (3): 271–84.

Pfister, J. (1996) 'The Americanization of cultural studies', in J. Storey (ed.), *What is Cultural Studies?: A Reader*. London: Arnold, pp. 287–300.

Pickering, M. (2009) (ed.) *Research Methods for Cultural Studies*. Edinburgh: Edinburgh University Press.

Potts, J. (2010) 'Do developing economies require creative industries? Some old theory about new China', *Chinese Journal of Communication*, 2 (1): 92–108.

Radway, J. (1984) *Reading the Romance: Women, Patriarchy and Popular Culture*. Chapel Hill, NC: University of North Carolina Press.

Radway. J. (1999) 'What's in a name?: Presidential address to the American Studies Association, 20 November 1998, *American Quarterly*, 51 (1): 1–32.

Radway, J., Gaines, K.K., Shanks, B. and Von Eschen, P. (eds) (2009) *American Studies: An Anthology*. Malden, MA: Wiley-Blackwell.

Sconce, J. (2003) 'Tulip theory' in J.T. Caldwell and A. Everett (eds), *New Media: Theories and Practices of Digitextuality*. New York: Routledge.

Shanks, B. (1997) 'The continuing embarrassment of culture: From the culture concept to cultural studies', *American Studies*, 38 (2): 95–116.

Shirky, C. (2008) *Here Comes Everybody: The Power of Organizing Without Organizations*. New York, NY: Penguin.

Shome, R. (2009) 'Postcolonial reflections on the "internationalization" of cultural studies', *Cultural Studies*, 23 (5–6): 694–719.

Shumway, D. (2010) 'When Institutions Haven't Been Built: Cultural Studies in the US', paper presented to the Cultural Crossroads conference of the Association of Cultural Studies, Hong Kong, June.

Sklar, R. (1975) 'The problem of an American studies' Philosophy: A bibliography of new direction', *American Quarterly*, 27: 245–62.

Slack, J.D. (1996) 'The theory and method of articulation in cultural studies' in D. Morley and K.K. Chen (eds), *Stuart Hall: Critical Dialogues in Cultural Studies*. London: Routledge, pp. 112–30.

Slack, J.D. (2005) 'Hope for the future: Cultural studies in the enclave', *Communication Review*, 8 (4): 393–404.

Stacey, J. (1993) *Star Gazing: Hollywood Cinema and Female Spectatorship*. London: Routledge.

Staiger, J. (1992) *Interpreting Films*. Princeton, NJ: Princeton University Press.

Staiger, J. (2000) *Perverse Spectators: The Practices of Film*. New York, NY: New York University Press.

Storey, J. (1996) (ed.) *What is Cultural Studies?: A Reader*. London: Hodder Arnold.

Stratton, J. and Ang, I. (1996) 'Towards the impossibility of a global cultural studies: "British" cultural studies in an "international" frame', in D. Morley and K.H. Chen (eds), *Stuart Hall: Critical Dialogues in Cultural Studies*. London: Routledge, pp. 361–91.

Striphas, T. (1998) 'Introduction. The long march: Cultural studies and its institutionalization', *Cultural Studies*, 12 (4): 453–75.

Tasker, Y. (1993) *Spectacular Bodies*. London: Routledge.

Taylor, L. (2006) 'Culture's revenge: Laurie Taylor interviews Stuart Hall; *The New Humanist*, 121: 2, March/April. Available at: http://newhumanist.org.uk/960/cultures-revenge-laurie-taylor-interviews-stuart-hall.

Thomas, N. (1999) 'Becoming undisciplined: Anthropology and cultural studies', in H. Moore (ed.), *Anthropological Theory Today*. Cambridge: Polity, pp. 262–79.

Turner, G. (1990) *British Cultural Studies: An Introduction*, 1st edn. London: Unwin Hyman Inc.

Turner, G. (1992) 'It works for me: British Cultural Studies, Australian Cultural Studies, Australian Film' in L. Grossberg, C. Nelson and P. Treichler (eds), *Cultural Studies*. New York, NY: Routledge, pp. 640–53.

Turner, G. (1993a) (ed.) *Nation, Culture, Text: Australian Cultural and Media Studies*. London: Routledge.

Turner, G. (1993b) 'Introduction. Moving the margins: Theory, practice and Australian cultural studies' in G. Turner (ed.), *Nation, Culture, Text: Australian Cultural and Media Studies*. London: Routledge, pp. 1–14.

Turner, G. (1996a) *British Cultural Studies: An Introduction*, 2nd edn. London: Routledge.

Turner, G. (1996b) '"Discipline Wars": Australian studies, cultural studies and the analysis of national culture', *Journal of Australian Studies*, 50: 6–17.

Turner, G. (2002) (ed.) *The Film Cultures Reader*. London: Routledge.

Turner, G. (2003) *British Cultural Studies: An Introduction*, 3rd edn. London: Routledge.

Turner, G. (2006) 'Informing the public: Is there a place for a critical humanities?' in *AAH Proceedings 2005*. Canberra: Australian Academy of the Humanities, pp. 131–41.

Turner, G. (2008a) 'Film and cultural studies' in J. Donald and M. Renov (eds), *The Sage Handbook of Film Studies*. London: Sage, pp. 270–83.

Turner, G. (2008b) 'Critical literacy, cultural literacy and the English school curriculum in Australia', in S. Owen (ed.), *Richard Hoggart and Cultural Studies*, London: Palgrave, pp. 158–70.

Turner, G. (2009a) 'Cultural studies 101: canonical, mystificatory and elitist', *Cultural Studies Review*, 15 (1): 175–87.

Turner, G. (2009b) 'Television and the nation: or doesn't this matter any-more?' in G. Turner and J. Tay (eds), *Television Studies after TV: Understanding Television in the Post-broadcast Era*. London: Routledge, pp. 54–64.

Turner, G. (2010) *Ordinary People and the Media: The Demotic Turn*. London: Sage.

Wang, J. (2004) 'The global reach of a new discourse: How far can "creative industries" travel?', *International Journal of Cultural Studies*, 7 (1): 9–20.

Willemen, P. (2010) 'A critical comment on the *IACS* journal', *Inter-Asia Cultural Studies*, 11 (2): 221–3.

Wolff, J. (1998) 'Cultural studies and the sociology of culture', in *Visible Culture: An Electronic Journal for Visual Studies* 1, Winter. Available at: http://www.rochester.edu/in_visible_culture/issue1/toc/toc.html (last accessed 25 February 2010).

INDEX